Michael Bristow is Asia/ World Service in London. He appears on radio and TV, commenting on developments in the world's fastest-changing region. Before that, he was a correspondent for the BBC in Beijing for five years, covering everything from earthquakes to the Olympics to the occasional outbreak of plague. He's been a journalist for more than 20 years, much of that time in East Asia, reporting not just from China, but from across the region, including Taiwan and North and South Korea. Apart from his family, China is his great passion, an interest that began while at university in Newcastle. He's spent much of his adult life trying to learn Mandarin, a task he imagines might take many more years. He lives in Yorkshire with his wife and their two children. This is his first book.

CHINA IN DRAG

Travels with a cross-dresser

Michael Bristow

SANDSTONEPRESS
HIGHLAND | SCOTLAND

Published in Great Britain by
Sandstone Press Ltd
Dochcarty Road
Dingwall
Ross-shire
IV15 9UG
Scotland.

www.sandstonepress.com

The publisher acknowledges support from Creative Scotland towards
publication of this volume.

ISBN: 978-1-910985-90-8
ISBNe: 978-1-910985-91-5

Cover design by David Wardle of Bold and Noble
Typeset by Iolaire Typesetting, Newtonmore
Printed and bound by Totem, Poland

*For Helen, who wouldn't let me stop writing this book,
and mostly for the teacher, a true friend.*

Contents

Prologue: A Revelation

The teacher didn't let me into his secret at the beginning. Even after we'd been friends for several years he kept it to himself. Perhaps he thought it was none of my business, or maybe he was worried about how I'd react. Whatever the reason, I'd known the teacher for about five years before he finally revealed the other side of his life. Looking back, I should perhaps have seen the signs, or at least wondered why he seemed a little different to other men of his age. He would sometimes turn up at our Chinese lessons with glowing lips that looked slightly pink. Was it lipstick? It was often cold outside and in Beijing's dry winter months it's not unusual to suffer from chapped skin, so I assumed that he was simply using a colourful balm. He'd also occasionally arrive at our lessons in a T-shirt that seemed far too tight for a man who was nearly sixty. His tops often had colourful logos emblazoned on the front that sparkled like the jewellery he sometimes wore.

His facelift should have given me another clue. I hadn't seen the teacher in a few weeks when he called out of the blue. I could barely hear his voice because it was so low, but over the course of several minutes, in which he spoke through obvious pain, he explained that he'd just had a facelift and not everything had gone according to plan. His face was fine; the problem was with the cut the plastic surgeon had made above the hairline. It wasn't healing properly and he felt intense pain with every move of his face and head. The teacher said he would have to cancel our lessons for a few months, until he'd recovered. When I finally did see him again, he was still making slow and deliberate movements, and hadn't washed his hair in a long time. I wondered why he'd had the facelift in the first place. It wasn't something you would expect from a man of his age, but I didn't want to ask. I decided that he would tell me if he wanted to.

How could I have missed the signs? In retrospect, it seems obvious that the teacher had a secret. The casual hints were perhaps his way of trying to tell me without having to spell it out. I'm a journalist for the BBC, I'm supposed to spot these things. The whole point of going to China was to observe the finer aspects of Chinese society. So, why wasn't I looking properly at the man in front of me? In my defence I'd say that, although the teacher and I met frequently, only occasionally did I suspect there was another part of his life that he hadn't let me into; the instances when I thought there was something he wasn't telling me were few and far between. But still...

The revelation finally came in Changsha, the capital of Hunan province. The day had been hot and we'd spent most of it on the road, travelling to various tourist sites. The city itself is like most others in modern China: on the move. For centuries, China's progress seemed to have stalled. Of course, there were remarkable developments. The country is credited with inventing gunpowder, paper and printing, and all are regularly mentioned by commentators who want to show how advanced Chinese civilisation at one time was. There's no question that China was once a great country, and is becoming so again, but in the few hundred years before the twentieth century momentum began to run out and the last emperor was finally unseated without much of a fight in 1911. Over the next few decades China suffered from colonial aggression, almost permanent civil war and unspeakable poverty for most of its people. Anyone would have been forgiven for thinking a great, ancient civilisation was almost gone, but modern China under the communist party is making up for lost time and things are changing quickly. In Changsha the pace was frenetic. As the teacher and I rode the bus into the city centre, we saw streets that had been ripped open to build a new subway system. It was like looking at the civil engineering equivalent of an operating table mid-way through a complicated procedure, with the patient waiting to be stitched back together. Cranes swung high above the rooftops as people rushed home from work and we headed to our hotel.

Although I'd known the teacher for a few years, this was the first time we'd been away together so I was a little nervous about how we'd get on. Were we sufficiently good friends to enjoy sustained periods of time together? More importantly, now we were standing before the hotel reception desk, should we share a room, which would be cheaper, or get one each? I decided to book two rooms and we left each other with an arrangement to meet again in the lobby at 8pm for dinner. I went to my room and the teacher went to his. I had a nap while he prepared his outfit for the night.

Just before eight, I opened my door, stepped into the corridor and looked towards the lift. The teacher was standing there, but something was different. It took me a second or two to realise what had changed: he'd dumped his usual shirt and trousers and now appeared before me wearing a smile and a full outfit of women's clothes. I paused for breath and took a good look. The teacher was dressed in a tight white T-shirt that clearly showed a bra underneath. It had glitzy silver writing on the front. He was also wearing matching white trousers. They were three-quarter length, which allowed me to glimpse the tights he'd pulled on. The teacher had obviously spent a long time doing his make-up.

He wore pink lipstick and light-blue eyeshadow, and had used a thick black pencil to trace the line of his eyebrows. He smiled and said: 'You don't mind, do you?' as he wafted a hand casually in the direction of his clothes. I didn't mind, but I was in shock. 'I think we probably need to talk about this,' was all I could mutter as we took the lift to the lobby.

I was in a daze as we stepped out of the hotel and into the glare of the colourful neon lights and signs that brighten Chinese streets at night. We walked along the pavement looking for a restaurant, attracting quizzical looks from passers-by. The question on their lips was not hard to read in their eyes: why was an elderly Chinese man dressed in women's clothes walking along with a younger Western man? I'm ashamed to admit that in those first few minutes I was a little embarrassed, and more than once when I caught the eye of someone staring at us I'd sigh and look at my travelling companion as if to say, 'All this has absolutely nothing to do with me.' It was the difference between theory and practice. In theory, I considered myself to be a tolerant person. I was surely someone who judged people on who they were, not on their race, gender or sexual orientation? I'd laboured under the misguided view that it wouldn't matter what a friend wore in my company. But if all that were true, why was I embarrassed?

The teacher gave no indication that he knew what I was thinking. He was enjoying himself. He'd occasionally stop to ask someone if they knew a good restaurant or what there was to see in Changsha. Every now and then he would turn to admire his reflection as we passed shop windows. Eventually, after a perilous journey across a footbridge, over which he struggled in his high-heeled shoes, we found somewhere to eat. When the food came, I settled down to hear the story of a cross-dressing Chinese pensioner.

The Teacher's Indestructible Scholar Tree

The story of the teacher's life didn't begin with the ability to walk down a street in a dress without worrying about what other people might think. The courage to do that came only later in life – and I found out about it even later still. At first, the teacher was nothing more to me than a tutor. He would arrive at my home two or three times a week to walk me through the complexities of a language that dates back thousands of years. We talked, we laughed and slowly we became friends. Later, we'd meet in a coffee shop off Beijing's Jianguomen Street after I'd cycled my son to school. The teacher never drank coffee himself; he would nurse a cup of hot water for an hour as he dispensed his opinions on the latest national events. Almost without noticing, the teacher's importance to my understanding of what was going on in China began to grow. He'd usually be able to add a story from his own life to whatever I was reporting on for the BBC. More often than not he would have a handy example of a problem he'd overcome, a difficulty he'd got around or pleasure he'd enjoyed.

Gradually, one anecdote at a time, I learned the story of his life. A schooling cut short by a disastrous political campaign, a spell in exile in the cold northeast and his first job, in a factory making monosodium glutamate. Along the way there were victories and disappointments. He found a wife, had a child and turned poverty into comfortable retirement. Slowly, I began to realise that this mostly scruffy, ageing man – whose face was still wrinkled despite the surgery – was the embodiment of modern China.

Don't get me wrong, in the grand sweep of human history the teacher is no one in particular. He's just one of 1.4 billion people who make up China's enormous population. He's never held a position of authority in China, or anywhere else, and has contributed little to the sum of knowledge that's slowly enlarged with each generation. The jobs he's done might seem mundane to an outside observer and now he's retired he has little energy, except for the effort needed to enjoy a reasonably comfortable life. The teacher is Mr Nobody or Mr Everybody, depending on your point of view. 'I can't be bothered to do anything apart from watch TV, surf the internet and eat,' he said shortly before I left China. He was exaggerating, but I knew what he meant. He was giving voice to the fact that he'd done and seen enough, like so many others of his generation.

I found his life both interesting and instructive. He was born in 1951, two years after the Chinese Communist Party came to power. The fortunes and direction of the country the party still governs have veered sharply in that time, and the teacher's life has mirrored those ups and downs. That's why I had the idea of writing his story in the first place. To retell the life of this one man is to reveal the story of China under the communist party. Thankfully, the teacher agreed to tell me what he'd done and what he knew. We decided to travel across China to the places that had played a part in his life story, so I could see things as well as hear them. The teacher also seemed to fancy a few trips away from Beijing, but to begin with he wanted to show me something closer to home, something that's central to his life story: a tree.

I didn't have far to travel. From where I was living, the tree is located just six subway stops across the heart of Beijing in the city's bustling financial district, Fuxingmen. The area has been transformed over recent years. It's now home to banks and multinational companies, and the fancy restaurants and five-star hotels that service their besuited employees. It's a place of giant tower blocks, built with impressive lobbies that suggest wealth and success. But not so long ago, before China shook off its communist shackles and embraced capitalism, Fuxingmen was a run-down neighbourhood of traditional Chinese houses: walled compounds with rooms arrayed around a central courtyard. I went there to look at what was left of the teacher's childhood home.

I met him at the spot where one of Beijing's most famous streets, the Avenue of Eternal Peace, would have entered the old city walls if they had still been there. The walls were knocked down decades ago to make way for increased traffic and the city's subway system, in what surely must rank as one of the worst decisions in the history of town planning. Instead of an ancient stone wall, a tacky multi-coloured archway greeted commuters making their way into the city centre from Fuxingmen. As I stood waiting, I tried to imagine the meeting at which communist planners had decided to tear down the old walls. A number of people had objected, but ultimately those voices had been silenced in the name of progress. An elderly Chinese friend once told me that his father, not usually given to public displays of emotion, had cried as he'd watched demolition workers pull down one particular section near his home. The communists destroyed walls in towns and cities across China, although ironically some are now being rebuilt. Local leaders have realised that tourists love them. Even in Beijing, the few remaining bits of wall that escaped the wrecking ball are now lovingly protected.

I also started thinking about the street's name, and how the events that began there on the night of 3rd June 1989 make a mockery of the words 'eternal peace'. It was on this avenue that soldiers gunned down students and residents when they ended the protests in Tiananmen Square. The Avenue of Mass Murder or the Street of Shot-Dead Students would surely be a more apt name for this central thoroughfare of death. But no, the name was about eternal peace. Like many things in communist China, the truth is often obscured. As I was contemplating these thoughts I saw the teacher shuffling along, a grin plastered across his face. He was clutching a new 'man bag', an accessory that had recently become fashionable.

I'd not had breakfast so I suggested stopping off at a McDonald's that had opened in a nearby shopping centre. The teacher agreed but seemed nervous, choosing seats far away from anyone else. It was the first day of our project to write his life story and he appeared to think someone might be watching us. Like most Chinese people, the teacher is willing to talk about many things in private, but in public he's more cautious. I dismissed his worries. I found it hard to believe that anyone would be spying on an elderly teacher and his student eating an unhealthy breakfast in the basement of a department store. Even the most daring of crime writers would surely shy away from turning that ordinary scene into the dramatic opening of a fast-paced thriller. But it says something of the teacher's state of mind and the country he lives in. The past, particularly the recent past, is still a sensitive subject in China and people are not encouraged to look back. Even the retelling of an ordinary life would require an investigation into some unsavoury episodes of China's recent history, and the teacher was a little unsettled.

After breakfast he seemed to forget his fears as we made our way north to the site of his old home. The district looked new and I wondered what would be left of the Alley of One

Hundred Children, where he had grown up. Had I thought about it for a few minutes, I could have easily guessed the answer to that question. Just like the city walls, the teacher's old house and the narrow alleyways that once riddled the area no longer exist. Of course, the teacher knew that all along. He hadn't taken me there to see his old home; he'd taken me to look at one of three trees from his childhood. This first one, tall and solid, is a Chinese scholar tree. It had formerly been the focal point at the centre of his courtyard home.

The tree has a trunk that splits into two at the bottom, so it's difficult to tell whether it's just one tree or two. The courtyard that it originally stood in was destroyed in the early 1990s when the new financial district started to take shape, but the developers left the tree untouched. It now sits among shrubbery outside the entrance to a modern office block, adding a dash of colour and life to the cold concrete of the building. A small green plaque with the words 'ancient tree' etched on has been nailed to the trunk. Attached to a low steel fence surrounding the tree, there's a forbidding sign that warns passers-by not to sit, lean or linger. I wondered why.

Looking round, I could see nothing but concrete and cars and people rushing to work. In that urban jungle of man-made materials the tree was one of the few indications that the natural world exists somewhere beyond the city limits. It would have surely been more fitting if the sign had encour-aged people to pause for a few moments and consider the beauty of nature. In any case, the warning proved unneces-sary; while we were there most workers hurried by, hardly glancing at the massive trunk lurking at the doorway of their place of work.

As we approached the tree through a car park, I became aware that we were being watched by a security guard who was dressed, as they inevitably are in China, in a uniform several sizes too large. With unskilled labour still relatively cheap, most offices and housing complexes have guards at their entrance or main gate. Many are young, fresh-faced men from the countryside with gentle, innocent faces. I seldom passed by one without wondering exactly what kind of security situation they could handle. They are usually quite diligent, or at least nosy, and two men poking around the bushes in front of an office block housing international companies were bound to attract attention. 'We're looking at a tree,' seemed an all-too-unsatisfactory response to the inevitable question about what game we were playing.

As it turned out the question never came. No one seemed to notice when the teacher slowly walked up to the tree and gave it a friendly pat, all the time looking up and down to check it was exactly as he remembered. The tree had what looked like Sellotape wrapped around its middle and a large hole in the trunk had been filled with cement; running repairs, no doubt, for past problems. But the teacher didn't seem to notice as he began to trace out the floor plan of his childhood home. The tree was in the centre of the courtyard; to the north there were four small rooms, with two more to the west. A further couple of rooms were added along the eastern side in the 1970s. Foreigners often find it difficult to understand China's changing society. They know little about what it was like before. But it's sometimes also hard to fathom for those who live there and are trying to make sense of what all the current upheaval means, if it means anything at all. The past might have been an unhappy place for many Chinese people, but it's where they grew up and shaped who they are today, and occasionally it's necessary to return there to see who they once were. That's why the teacher goes back to visit his tree at least once a year. He wants to be reminded of where he came from.

The tree has witnessed many of the political changes of the last hundred years. The courtyard home it once sheltered was given to the teacher's grandfather by his boss, who ran a rickshaw business. He was a capitalist, to use the derogatory language once employed by China's communist rulers. It was a fact that meant the teacher never quite believed government officials when they criticised the old economic order and those who had benefited from it. If businessmen had been so bad, what set of circumstances had led one of them to give his grandfather a house? The teacher's parents eventually inherited the home. He describes them as having 'no culture'. Though loving, the teacher is like many other Chinese people: brutally honest. His father repaired cars, while his mother worked in a factory making parts for them. With his three brothers and one sister, the teacher's first few years beneath the ancient scholar tree were pleasant and undisturbed.

The tree was not simply a passive observer of history: it occasionally played a leading role. In 1958 Mao Zedong launched a hygiene campaign to eradicate four pests: mosquitoes, flies, rats and sparrows. Of the four, it seems sparrows were least able to withstand this onslaught. Mao thought they ate too much grain, so people across the country were instructed to kill them. Loyal citizens stood beneath trees banging pots and pans and shouting at the top of their voices, to stop the poor sparrows from resting in the branches. Eventually, the exhausted birds would fall to the floor. If they were not already dead they'd be beaten to death. The teacher's scholar tree was the biggest in the neighbourhood and so became a rallying point for the campaign to eradicate the birds. People would come home from work and head to his courtyard to do a shift of sparrow killing, which went on day and night. Of course, the campaign did not last long, only until the authorities realised that without sparrows to kill them, insects were free to multiply and attack the country's crops. Instead of increasing grain yields as Chairman Mao had hoped, the killing meant production fell and so the remaining birds were spared. 'The campaign to kill the sparrows was like a gust of wind blowing through – and like a gust of wind it soon blew away,' was how the teacher spoke of that time afterwards.

These mass public campaigns to cleanse the country of unwanted pests continue today. A few years ago, Beijing city government was responsible for perhaps one of the more bizarre. It issued a new standard for all public toilets that stipulated they could contain no more than two flies at any one time. The directive left many questions unanswered, not least of which was how officials would ensure the new rule was being observed. Would an army of flycatchers be sent to roam the city's lavatories? What were they to do if they found more than two flies in any one toilet? There's no doubt something needed to be done about Beijing's public conveniences. Residents can usually smell them before they see them and they are seldom cleaned, if we are to stick with the common definition of the verb 'to clean'. Occasionally, someone will drag a dirty grey mop across a toilet floor, but that only seems to move the muck from one place to another. How is it that a nation that brought us so many inventions long before anyone else had managed to underplay the advantages of a hygienic place to poo?

In keeping with the times, the teacher's childhood home had no flush toilet. It didn't even have a toilet. But his tree did have a walk on part in another momentous event in modern Chinese history. When a massive earthquake struck the city of Tangshan in the summer of 1976 hundreds of thousands of people died. It was so big that tremors were felt in Beijing, more than 100 miles away, and like everyone else in the capital the teacher and his family rushed outside when the walls started to shake. Fortunately, they had somewhere safe to shelter: underneath their immoveable scholar tree. In the hours that followed, the teacher's father sawed off branches and used them to build a makeshift shelter beneath the tree, much to the envy of neighbours who had to camp out in the streets, worried about things falling on their heads.

Sometimes the tree also seemed to reflect the mood of the times. During the political upheaval of the Cultural Revolution the world was turned upside down and chaos reigned in the streets, as Mao sought to reassert his control over the country. The teacher thinks the tree seemed to know what was going on because signs of death and decay started to take hold. Buds came late in the spring of 1967, and never came at all to some of the top-most branches. The tree was then infested with a plague of 'hangman bugs' that ate all the leaves. There were so many insects that they would drop into the teacher's rice bowl as he sat underneath to eat his meals. There was no properly functioning government in China at the time, so there was no one to call for help. Eventually, the family decided to cut off some of the most infested branches and that seemed to work. The tree returned to normal. The stumps of some of those cut-off branches are still visible today and the teacher happily told me the story of the bugs while prodding one of them, ignoring the sign that warned us not to linger.

It was clear from our visit that the teacher loved his tree in a way that I'd never contemplated before. Sometime later he sent me an article he'd written about it. I translated his writing and was struck afresh by the tenderness he felt towards a trunk and a few branches that grow, mostly unnoticed, outside the entrance to an ordinary-looking office block. In the piece, he spoke about the day his tree was marked out as important...

One day in the 1980s some workmen from the parks' department came to our home and nailed a sign to the tree. One of them said it was 'ancient' and we should take good care of it. He said it was rare to see trees like this that grow together, particularly Chinese scholar trees. These few words made me extremely sad because I realised that in the past we hadn't looked after the tree very well. I promised that I would do so in the future and so, at my suggestion, the family cleared away all the clutter that had gathered around the base of the tree. Every day I would clean it. I also pruned the branches. I made up for the mistreatment of the past.

When the time came for the family to leave their courtyard home to make way for the new financial district, the teacher realised he didn't want to say goodbye to the tree...

Our family moved on, but the tree couldn't come with us. It now had a sign to say it was one of the nation's natural resources. But I was reluctant to part forever with something that we'd lived with for decades. When I thought about the tree's fate, there were three possibilities. One, I could take it with us. Two, I could chop it down or three, it could remain as the centrepiece of a garden, so people could gaze upon it forever.

Many years have now passed since I left my life with the tree. My new spacious home is far better than the previous courtyard, but every time I go back to Fuxingmen and stand under the old tree my heart flies back to the courtyard home of my memories, to the tree that had shared my younger, simpler life.

The teacher's childhood home is not the only thing that has gone from Fuxingmen. There is little in the immediate neighbourhood to remind the world of how the area once used to look. The city walls have been demolished, other courtyard homes have been torn down and even the street layout has changed. One section of an ancient temple complex remains, but the squat red building is now surrounded by towering blocks of concrete, steel and glass. It looks out of place, like a bent old man among a crowd of youngsters. The same transformation has happened in countless other Beijing districts, and in countless other towns and cities across China, leaving former residents unable to find the landmarks of their past. For the teacher, only trees give a hint as to what the area was like before. He'd already shown me the scholar tree, now he wanted me to see two more.

We trudged back to the department store where we had eaten that nervous breakfast, but this time went around the back. There, among a pile of odds and ends that included an old mop, bags of sand and an assortment of concrete slabs, were two ginkgo trees. The department store looked as if it had been built around them. Once again, a sign saying 'ancient tree' had been nailed to each trunk and both trees had been fenced off. Someone, somewhere, must once have thought it necessary to preserve these trees but here, in the middle of winter with their branches shorn of leaves, they looked forlorn and forgotten. Previously, they'd stood in the sprawling courtyard residence, now long gone, of a once-famous scholar called Yu Pingbo. The teacher had gone to the primary school that had been set up in the academic's home; that's why he wanted me to visit this spot.

I knew nothing of Yu Pingbo when I went to see the two trees. The teacher mentioned that he'd been an expert on one of China's most famous works of literature, the eighteenth-century novel *The Dream of the Red Chamber*, and that he had been persecuted during the Cultural Revolution, but he said little else. Later, I looked up the man who had allowed part of his home to become a school. His story is just one of millions that reveal the madness that has occasionally erupted in China. This mania sometimes comes from an unlikely source. In this case, it had been Yu Pingbo's research into the *Red Chamber* novel that had landed him in trouble. In communist China, even the pages of an old book can cause a political scandal centuries after its publication.

Yu Pingbo was a writer and academic whose career began at the birth of modern China, following the fall of the last emperor in 1911. He wrote poetry, but it seems his work on *The Dream of the Red Chamber* was what really fired him up. The book tells the story of the decline and fall of the Jia family. Its central character is a young man destined to head the clan, but it also details the lives of dozens of other people and how they lived during China's last imperial dynasty, the Qing. Yu Pingbo spent decades researching the book and seems to have come to a couple of conclusions that at first sight do not seem particularly contentious. He decided that the author, Cao Xueqin, had written only the first 80 chapters of the book and not the final 40. He also believed it was nothing more than the autobiographical tale of the man who penned it. It was this last conclusion that got him into trouble.

To understand why such a view might be contentious you have to understand the thinking of China's early communists. In their opinion, a writer was not someone who could be left alone to produce whatever he or she wanted, and a novel was not simply something pleasant to read on the sofa after work. All art, including literature, had to help bring about a socialist transformation, and all artists ultimately had to work for the party and its political goals. Even novels written long before Karl Marx had drawn his first breath had to be understood in Marxist terms. The communists believed *The Dream of the Red Chamber* was a book that not only reflected the decline of the Jia family, but of Chinese society as a whole. They thought the novel should be seen as an attack on the corrupt Qing court and its officials, and was not simply the story of one family's troubles.

Yu Pingbo disagreed and in 1954 faced a barrage of criticism, even from Chairman Mao himself. He had to endure hostile meetings at which he was accused of failing to reform his bourgeois outlook. In the twisted world of 1950s China the party tried to reform those who displayed the 'wrong' kind of thinking. It was not enough that people accepted its right to rule; they also had to see the world from its point of view, and sometimes that required a bit of persuasion. Yu Pingbo was accused of the ridiculous-sounding charge of looking into small details for the sake of looking into small details, and failing to see the big picture.

The two students who initially criticised him – no doubt with the approval of senior party officials – claimed *The Dream of the Red Chamber* was obviously a portent of the coming collapse of 'the feudal, bureaucratic landlord class under the new historical conditions that were being formed'. Such out-dated ideological language now seems almost quaint, but back then it had real power to destroy lives. Yu Pingbo managed to survive the attack on his reputation in the 1950s, but further persecution in the Cultural Revolution a decade or so later shows he was probably never trusted again. He was an academic whose opinions were not in tune with the mood of the times and that was a dangerous thing.

As I read about the scholar's story I came across a fragment of a letter he had written to a friend, more than three decades before he felt the full force of communist thought control. In it he laid out his views about the book he obviously loved. 'I believe that what the author of *The Dream of the Red Chamber* wants to say is nothing else but that he began with a life of happiness, but ended in a rather miserable state. He painfully recollects his life and is nostalgic about his previous joys.' Perhaps Yu Pingbo could have applied those words to his own life. And what about the teacher? It's an exaggeration to say that he's miserable, but there is certainly something wistful about his visits to the trees that were part of his childhood. Life for him is materially much better than it was before, but it's clear that he also occasionally, even painfully, recollects his own 'previous joys'.

If the teacher is nostalgic, he's not the only one. In China today most people have little time to think about the past as they are too busy building the future, but they do sometimes express a fondness for the era under Chairman Mao. There was an old-fashioned department store in southern Beijing where nostalgia was clearly on show. Most shoppers, at least those with money, now flock to the Western-style shopping centres that have sprung up across the Chinese capital. These sell designer goods and dreams of a happier, more comfortable life ahead, but at the Yong'an Road Department Store, established in 1958, they sold something entirely different: the past. When I visited, it stocked the cheap, Chinese-made consumer goods that were the only things to buy when the communist party was still trying to be communist. The shelves were jammed with items such as slip-on cloth shoes, the kind worn by kung-fu masters; enamel cups; and faded posters of Mao, usually surrounded by a group of smiling workers. Some shoppers went there because they didn't have the money to go elsewhere, but others trudged across the capital to buy the products they remembered from their youth. Their faces lit up at the smell of forgotten face creams and the rattle of cheap, tin kitchenware.

Back behind the Fuxingmen department store, as we stared at the two ginkgo trees and were in turn watched by a bemused man selling newspapers, I couldn't help feeling a little depressed. Chinese courtyards represent some of

18

the most beautiful architecture ever created: elegant tiled roofs, pillars of wood painted red and an imaginative use of space. They have a symmetry that has served for centuries as a template for homes, palaces and monasteries. A poor labourer could sleep in a place that in design would not be dissimilar to the rooms in which the emperor lay his anointed head. These two trees must have once graced a magnificent courtyard, but looking at them now it's almost impossible to imagine what that home must have looked like. The fence around the trees had originally been painted white, but had long since rusted. The department store, only a few years old, was already showing signs of age. The building had been clad on the outside with cheap, steel panels; black goo had started to seep from between some of them. A large poster showing a close-up of a woman's face had been stuck onto a back window. It was probably an advert for a brand of cosmetics. The model's cool, modern stare made it impossible to imagine what this space had previously looked like. It only added to my sense of melancholy.

It wasn't unusual to come across such scenes of architectural desolation in China. In the rush to modernise, planners have given the go-ahead to thousands of ill-thought-out and poorly executed projects. The memory of two places in particular will forever send a shudder down my spine; one is a square, the other is a room. My wife and I would refer to the former by the Chinese word for 'square'. To us, it was known simply and with foreboding as the *guangchang*. In truth it wasn't much of a square, just a patch of concrete that hadn't been built upon. It was round the back of a compound that housed the *China Daily*, an English-language newspaper in Beijing where both of us worked for a while as sub-editors. We used to take our young son to the *guangchang*. It was somewhere for him to run around and he'd occasionally go on one of the creaky children's rides that were tucked away in one corner, next to a food stall where a man with a filthy apron would sell sausages on sticks.

We found it difficult to put our finger on just what it was about the place that made it so depressing. Was it the pollution that usually hung over the pensioners who'd shuffle around the square? Was it the constant noise of traffic from a nearby intersection? Or was it the shadow of Roman Gardens, a once-posh-now-dilapidated housing complex that towered over the area? Roman Gardens had at one time attracted Beijing's wealthier residents, but ever since newer more desirable homes had been built its apartments could only be sold for rock-bottom prices. It seemed a metaphor for everything that could go wrong with China's capitalist reforms. Whatever it was that caused our gloom, we would always return from the *guangchang* slightly subdued. If the aim had been to lift our spirits by getting out into the open, it usually failed.

Unlike the square, I saw the room only once, but its bleakness is seared into my memory banks. It was nothing much to speak of, little more than an antechamber that opened onto the stage of a meeting room. Communist dignitaries would wait there for a few minutes and collect their thoughts before striding out to give a speech. It was in the municipal offices of a small county in the west of China. I spent no more than an hour in there as I waited for a local government official to finish talking. Like the *guangchang*, I found it hard to work out exactly why the room filled me with so much dread. After all, there had been some attempt at elegance. The room contained two easy chairs with tasselled covers and between them sat a small table holding two tea cups, but there had been little attempt to make the room warm and inviting. No one had bothered to wash the chair covers in a long time and there was a thick layer of dust on the table.

The concrete walls had been painted with a thin lime-green wash, which gave the place an eerie glow. There were dirty hand marks all over the walls, as though someone had been attempting to scale them in a desperate bid to escape. Bits of wall had been chipped off, no doubt through years of use and carelessness, revealing the grey concrete beneath. The room was uncarpeted and cold, and apart from the table and chairs there was nothing else in there. It wasn't a place to inspire anything, least of all a well-delivered and moving speech.

In order to break the grim silence behind the department store, I asked the teacher what kind of pupil he'd been. I already knew the answer. Anyone who takes the time to come back and look at two trees from a long-gone school-yard must have a great deal of affection for the place, and so it turned out. The teacher loved school from an early age. 'I wanted to be a scientist,' he told me, as he picked over the various items that had been discarded near the two trees. He won a maths contest, beating children far older than him. He became interested in making things, working out that if he hung an aerial in the top branches of his own tree he would get a better reception on the family radio.

The teacher's timing was wrong. The optimism of the early years of communist party rule began to crumble as the leadership disagreed about how to move forward. Did they need more, or less, communism? Mao decided they needed more and that signalled the beginning of the end for the teacher's pleasant childhood beneath the Chinese scholar tree in the Alley of One Hundred Children. The attack on Yu Pingbo was a foretaste of the madness just around the corner. One morning in May 1966 at about 11am, when the teacher was in his first year of middle school, there was an announcement over the school's public address system. Chairman Mao had launched his oddly titled Great Proletarian Cultural

Revolution. The children's teacher told them to ignore the announcement and get back to work; it meant nothing. He didn't know it at the time, but it was to be the teacher's last day at school. It would be nearly two decades before he could pick up his studies again and begin fulfilling some of those early dreams.

Gulag Revisited

As our train trundled northwards, carving its way through the smog that seems to hang almost permanently over much of China, an elderly woman reached for a copy of the *People's Railway Daily* that had been delivered free to our compartment. I was surprised because it was the first time I'd actually seen anyone pick up this dour publication, which documents the life of China's rail network. Rolling stock and passenger numbers do not easily lend themselves to catchy headlines and interesting stories. Worse still, the paper is run by the railways ministry, which weeds out all the potentially embarrassing – and so interesting – stories about corruption, crashes and intrigue on the iron rails. The newspaper is usually displayed in carriages on trains travelling throughout China, but it mostly just sits there, unread and neatly folded, in its rack.

This particular edition had tried to entice readers with a front-page photograph of two attractive female guards helping an elderly passenger off a train, but to little effect. The newspaper in our compartment was as crisp as the moment it had come off the printing press. Even the woman who picked it up did not want to read about the two attendants and their exemplary service. Without bothering to pause over headlines declaring the latest achievements brought to China's train-travelling public, she pulled the newspaper apart and laid it neatly on the floor.

She was travelling with her husband and their two-year-old grandson, naked from the waist down and not yet toilet trained. After she'd laid out the newspaper, and with no warning for those sharing the cramped compartment, the grandmother picked up the youngster, pulled apart his legs and encouraged him to open his bowels onto the newsprint. He did. For 15 minutes. The grandfather got up and left the compartment, gently closing the door behind him so as not to disturb his grandson's efforts. I was left in the confined space trying to read my book as the toddler grunted and groaned his way through what was probably a nightly ritual. 'It's a little dry,' said the grandmother to her husband when he returned. The elderly gentleman peered down to take a look and I couldn't help but do the same. His wife was right. It was a little dry.

It was at moments like these that I'd wonder how I ended up in China in the first place. What sequence of events had led me to a small compartment halfway across the world in which a group of strangers were discussing the consistency of a child's turd? Until I'd gone to university I'd hardly travelled outside the small Yorkshire village in which I'd grown up. Had there been well-thought-out decisions along the way? Had there been clear signposts on my journey through life? The answer was no, embarrassingly so when I remember the original decision that had set me on the road to China. I'd only chosen to study East Asia at university in Newcastle because it promised a year abroad, a year away from Britain. And I'd been intending all along to go to Japan because in the 1980s Japan was the next big thing. Its companies were taking over the world and its well-dressed tourists could be spotted in every major capital. Few people thought much about China back then, a country that was still struggling to put right the mayhem caused by Mao.

I changed my mind, in an instant. It happened as I was on

my way to a university meeting at which I'd have to make a final decision about where I wanted to go in my year away. For no particular reason I remember it was raining. I was walking along with two fellow students who told me, with the clarity of people who appeared to have given the issue some thought, that I really ought to go to China because that was the more interesting country. They said it had potential and pretty soon everyone would want to know about it. They were right, but I had no way of knowing that then. It didn't seem to matter. Without a moment's hesitation I changed my plans. China it was. It turned out to be such a good choice that since then I've often considered outsourcing the major decisions of my life to other people.

Of course, a lot has happened since that decision on a rain-swept street in Newcastle and those awkward few moments in a Chinese train compartment, but most of the roads I've taken have at some point led back to China. Somewhere along the way my wife caught the same bug and so in our mid-thirties we decided to give up our jobs and take our eleven-month-old son to Beijing, to study Chinese and try to understand a country that many foreigners still find baffling. Henry Kissinger, the American politician who arranged the rapprochement between China and the United States in the 1970s, tells the story of how he once asked the Chinese leader, Zhou Enlai, why it was that his country and its people were so inscrutable. In an attempt to put right this misconception, Mr Zhou apparently turned to the American and said China was very simple to understand for the millions of Chinese people who lived there. I was in China because I wanted to understand too. My wife and I studied Chinese for two years in Beijing while working on the *China Daily*. I then found a job there with the BBC. I met the teacher and eventually decided to write his life story. In a roundabout way, that's how I found myself shut up in a

Chinese train compartment with a toddler who'd just been to the toilet.

The teacher and I were on our way to Qiqihar, a city in China's most northerly province of Heilongjiang, a vast wedge of land between Russia and Mongolia that for many months sits under snow and ice. The teacher was taking me to the small town of Double River Farm. It was not the first time he had travelled this route and not the first time he'd been to Double River Farm, although when he first went there it was known by a different name and his visit had nothing to do with pleasure. I was about to find out what had happened to the teacher when the chaos of the Cultural Revolution finally caught up with him. I was about to find out what had happened to him after his school life had suddenly stopped.

We boarded our train at Beijing Railway Station, one of ten great buildings constructed at the end of the 1950s to celebrate a decade of communist rule. Its vast, elegant waiting rooms, with their ornate chandeliers and intricate plasterwork, were built to showcase the achievements of what was then still a new government. That night, as is so often the case, the waiting room was crammed full of people who seemed impatient to get on with their journey. No one was looking up to admire the plasterwork. In China, passengers are usually forced to sit in station waiting rooms until just before the train is due to leave. Predictably, there's a mad rush when the call goes out to get on and the gates that guard the entrance to the platforms finally open. It was no different on the day I travelled north with the teacher. We managed to clamber aboard just moments before a whistle announced our departure.

As people pushed and shoved their way onto the train, the teacher pointed out that we were leaving from platform one, the same one he'd pulled away from when he'd first travelled to Double River Farm in September 1969. There had been more than a thousand other teenagers on board that first train, all of them in good spirits. As their train left Beijing on what had been a perfectly clear autumn day, it suddenly started to rain. The teenagers leaned out of the windows and waved goodbye to their parents, who'd come to see them off. The teacher said it had been a difficult goodbye, as it no doubt was for all those worried mothers and fathers. However good the propaganda underpinning the trip, they must have realised that their children were heading towards an unknown and uncertain future. Conditions were cramped. No one had a bed, just a hard wooden seat, but it didn't seem to matter because that first train ride had the feel of a school trip. 'I didn't cry when we left. I was happy to go,' the teacher recalled. 'We had answered Chairman Mao's call to go and learn from the peasants.'

The youngsters had very little with them, just a few clothes and a little money. They were given steamed buns and biscuits for the journey, but no one really wanted them. When the train stopped in railway sidings, as it did many times during its slow journey north, the teenagers threw them out of the windows. They laughed as hungry farmers outside scrambled to grab the food. The travellers didn't think they needed the buns or the biscuits because they'd been sent to the countryside by Chairman Mao and expected an enthusiastic welcome – and a large meal – when they got to Heilongjiang.

They were wrong to be so optimistic. When they arrived at Qiqihar they were quickly sent further north in trucks to Double River Farm, which was then run by the army and was nothing more than a military-style camp known simply as Company 56. Once there, the youngsters were given a meal of two steamed buns. Their initial enthusiasm quickly disappeared and on that first night in Heilongjiang more than a few began to cry. One boy tried to escape, walking for five hours to the nearest town before being brought back on a tractor by one of the camp's leaders. They were there to stay whether they liked it or not.

The teacher leaned back on his bunk opposite mine and relaxed. He'd been telling me the story of his first trip to Double River Farm as our own train wound its way along the same route. Unsurprisingly, he was in a thoughtful mood. As a teenager he may have been an enthusiastic believer in Mao's wisdom, but that faith had long since dissipated. Looking back from a distance of several decades, the teacher was as close to angry as I'd ever seen him. 'There are some things you never forget,' he said. 'What happened isn't just about me, but about a whole generation.' Outside the Chinese countryside flashed by. By this time the smog was hidden by the fast-advancing night. The two-year-old boy had fallen asleep. Thankfully, he was wearing a nappy so we were probably safe from toilet interruptions for at least a few hours. As the train gently swayed, the teacher's eyes slowly closed and we didn't pick up the thread of his story again that night. I was left to ponder alone what he had felt on that first trip to Double River Farm, as he'd headed towards a new life.

Qiqihar is a city of more than one million people, but has little to interest a passing tourist. My giant travel guide of China, big enough to double up as a doorstop, could find no room for this metropolis among its hundreds of pages. A gloom descended on me as we approached and the light rain that greeted our arrival seemed particularly suited to the city and my mood. The station is the most interesting building for miles around, but it was soon to be replaced as the city's main entry point. Another was being built to the south to accommodate a new high-speed rail line, a development that might allow this northern outpost to feel less remote. I wasn't surprised to learn that the old station was being discarded.

In modern China it's easier to sweep away the past and start again by building from scratch than to renovate something old. It looked as though no one had bothered to repair the original, dilapidated terminal in years. It seemed a shame to let it just fall apart.

The art deco station was built in 1934, just a few years after the Japanese had invaded this part of north-eastern China. They'd set up a puppet state called Manchukuo, which was nominally ruled by the man who'd been China's last emperor, Pu Yi, but it was really under the control of the Japanese army. The plaque at the front of the station made no mention of this foreign influence. I was thinking about that omission when I noticed another reminder of a long-gone era. On top of the station building the slogan 'Long live Mao Zedong Thought' was written in red Chinese characters ten-feet high. Communist China's founding father died in 1976, but someone in Qiqihar still seemed to love him.

The teacher didn't want to hang around. He was eager to go straight to Double River Farm, so we pushed through the rain and walked to the bus station for the last leg of our journey. We sat and waited for our departure among a cross section of the poorer parts of Chinese humanity, who'd stored their belongings in everything from fake designer bags to cardboard boxes. They looked as eager as we were to be on our way, although the owners of food stalls and knick-knack sellers were doing their best to delay them, in the hope that they would spend at least a little before boarding their buses.

I wandered around the bus station and came across a series of disturbing photographs hung along the wall nearest the entrance. They were graphic images of deadly traffic accidents that had scarred local roads over recent months. No detail had been left out in this warning against the possible consequences of poor driving. One photograph showed a three-wheeled motorised cart wedged under a large truck. The driver of the cart was still in his seat, obviously dead, with his head flipped backwards and an expression of agony on his face. I wondered why the authorities had bothered to put the pictures in the waiting room. After all, we were just passengers and wouldn't be driving. Surely the photographs would only serve to make us more anxious. It would have made far more sense to display them in the drivers' rest area. I was hoping our own man at the wheel had seen the pictures and taken in their grim message.

Double River Farm is a couple of hours' drive from Qiqihar. The road runs arrow straight, with tall trees on both sides masking fields of wheat, maize and rice. The town itself is not much to look at: one main street lined with shops, restaurants and market stalls. Small one-storey homes have been built along narrow lanes that run at right angles off the main street. It reminded me of the kind of town you might find on a Hollywood film set of America's Wild West: it was all front, with nothing much behind. It's a drab place, particularly in the rain, but the teacher was excited because so much had changed since he was last there. Shops sold everything from veterinary medicine to high-heeled shoes, although I couldn't help wondering where people wore such footwear. There were no pavements to speak of, just puddles of mud, and for much of the winter the town is blanketed in snow. But it was clear that Double River Farm was thriving. It even had a night school offering English classes. It hadn't been like that during the teacher's six years there. At that time, there was only one shop and that didn't sell much.

When he left Beijing in the autumn of 1969, the teacher was just one of millions of young people from all across China who were being sent 'up to the mountains and down to the countryside', as the misleadingly pleasant-sounding slogan of the time put it. It was a campaign dreamed up by China's

leader Mao Zedong, who said he wanted the country's teenagers to learn from those who tilled the land. He thought
a few years working in the fields might make them more
communist. But this explanation was to a large extent just a
cover story to excuse his decision to part so many youngsters
from their homes and families. At the start of the Cultural
Revolution, Mao had whipped up the nation's young people
into a frenzy of political activity. Teenagers formed bands
of Red Guards, who roamed the streets and engaged in an
orgy of destruction. People, homes, institutions and even
traditions came under attack. The Chairman's rivals – some
of the country's top leaders – were forced to endure lengthy
sessions of public criticism, sometimes in front of crowds of
thousands of snarling youngsters, who humiliated and even
tortured their victims. But the Red Guards soon became a
liability, bringing disorder to the entire country. Normal life
was suspended as schools, factories and hospitals closed or
were severely disrupted. The Red Guards then began to fight
among themselves. To control these unruly young people
Mao sent them to the countryside, where they could do less
damage and where their energies might be directed towards
more productive projects.

I wanted to know what the teacher had done to be sent
away. Nothing, was his answer. He told me he hadn't joined
the Red Guards in 1966 when the Cultural Revolution began
because he'd been too young. Did I believe him? I had no
choice, and he did admit that he'd been caught up in the
mood of the times. Mao greeted millions of youngsters at
several enormous rallies in Beijing's Tiananmen Square, and
the teacher was one of those who went along. With no school
and no role in the Red Guards, he spent much of the late
1960s kicking his heels. He would go to work with his father
or build things at home, but he was mostly bored. He was sent
away anyway, along with all those other youngsters who'd

been rampaging through the streets. The teacher was told to leave Beijing and given three possible destinations: Yunnan, Inner Mongolia and Heilongjiang. He chose the latter. A troop of children from his old school, banging drums and crashing cymbals, came round to his home to confirm the news. 'Congratulations, you're being sent to a military unit in the northeast!' they shouted. It was as though the teacher had just won the first prize in a competition.

The teacher was taking me to Heilongjiang because he wanted to return to where he'd spent so much of his young life, quarrying stone and planting crops when he should have been sitting behind a school desk. Surprisingly, ours wasn't a journey of bitterness and regret at all those wasted years. When we pulled out of Beijing Railway Station on our way north, the teacher was as joyful as he'd been on that first trip to Double River Farm. It was as if he were revisiting a childhood holiday destination that held only fond memories.

Double River Farm is not like other towns, something I noticed when we first arrived on its outskirts, where a barrier blocked the road. It was as if we were entering another domain. A giant roadside poster in the town itself offered another clue. It said: 'Build a humane Beijing, a scientific Beijing and a green Beijing.' What had a small town in Heilongjiang province got to do with the Chinese capital, hundreds of miles away to the south? The teacher told me that Double River Farm had long been administered by Beijing – apart from a brief period during the Cultural Revolution when it was run by the military – and one city department in particular had been responsible for this enclave: the Beijing Re-education Through Labour Work Management Bureau. It's a long-winded title for an organisation with an unsavoury reputation.

'Re-education through labour' feels like a phrase that belongs to a bygone era, when totalitarian governments attempted to re-engineer the thinking of those they considered politically suspect. But in China the authorities are only slowly giving up on the idea of sending people away to have their thinking reformed. Re-education was introduced soon after the communists took control in 1949 and was a form of punishment that existed largely outside the normal criminal justice system. It allowed the police to send away low-level criminals – thieves, prostitutes and troublemakers – for up to four years without trial. No one was beyond punishment.

During the Beijing Olympics in 2008 two elderly women were threatened with a year's re-education because they complained about being rehoused. The fact that one was partially blind and both walked with the aid of sticks did not mean they were exempt from punishment. This system was also used to silence dissidents and activists. In 2013, China announced it was closing these camps, but there's evidence to suggest that many institutions simply changed their names and focused on reforming people with specific problems, such as drug addiction. Chinese leaders have certainly not given up on the idea of getting disruptive people to see life from their point of view. By the time I visited, the authorities had stopped sending offenders to Double River Farm, but the prison facilities were still well maintained. It was as though someone thought they might be needed again at some point in the future.

The teacher and I wandered the streets, bumping into people whose destinies had been shaped by trivial acts carried out several decades before, often by other family members. One of those people served us pork dumplings, our first meal in the town. As we ravenously tucked into her cooking, the woman who ran the restaurant told us she'd been born in Double River Farm in 1970, a few years after her father had been sent there for shouting an insult at a newspaper photograph of Mao Zedong. The woman's own children had also been born in the town. The significance of this story hit me only after I'd polished off my food: three generations blighted by one minor transgression nearly half a century ago. It was a small crime, but a punishment that had not yet ended.

I felt sad when I heard her story, but the teacher wasn't really listening. It's not that he wasn't sympathetic; he'd just heard it all before. For him, it was too commonplace to be news. When he'd bolted down his food he was keen to be off, to find an old friend who had shared his hardships during the Cultural Revolution. The friend had been sent to Double River Farm at the same time as everyone else, but he'd never left. His parents were already dead by the time Mao's disastrous political campaign ended and the millions of 'educated youth', as the youngsters sent to the countryside were known, began drifting home. The friend saw no point in going back as he had nothing to go back for, so he stayed in Double River Farm, got married and had a daughter.

When we found his house, the teacher was puzzled by the presence of a woman who was not his friend's wife. Three years earlier, when the teacher had first re-established contact with his friend, he'd still been married. But since then he had split up with his wife and moved in with this younger woman. She was fifty and had wild, unkempt hair that was grey at the roots. She had a habit – a good one I thought for such a harsh place – of always laughing. I noticed that the four fingers on her right hand were missing, an annoyance that did not impair her ability to smoke. When she lit up at dinner that night she clutched her cigarette between two stumps. She told me the fingers had been cut off one day as she'd been feeding maize stalks into a machine that chopped them into animal feed. It had a rotating blade and in a moment's loss of concentration she'd found out just how sharp it was. 'Suddenly my fingers were gone,' she said, taking another drag on her cigarette and inadvertently showing me her stumps again.

As we ate and drank, she became more talkative and started telling me about the anger felt by some of the people living in Double River Farm. Life has improved over recent years, but some residents felt they had not benefited enough from the country's economic boom. Many older people said their pensions were too small and some had even decided to take their complaints to Beijing, where they could explain their position to a higher level of government. But the pensioners' most recent trip to the capital had not been a success. They hadn't even managed to get there because the authorities had kidnapped them at bus and railway stations along the way and brought them back. 'There's nothing we can do,' shrugged the woman with the missing fingers. Her nonchalance suggested state-sanctioned thuggery is nothing out of the ordinary in that part of China.

It's common in other regions too. The pensioners from Double River Farm were attempting a journey to Beijing that's made every year by thousands of others from across the country. They take with them documents that detail perceived injustices meted out by corrupt local officials. It's embarrassing for both local leaders, who might have to explain themselves, and the central government, which does not want bands of dissatisfied citizens roaming the streets of the capital. Many local authorities hire private security firms to stop these people getting to Beijing, or kidnap them and bring them home if they do manage to make it that far. The story of the pensioners from Double River Farm is nothing unusual. I'd heard similar things before, and as the woman with the missing fingers spoke I remembered the tale of Zhou Zhipei, whose distressing story had once captured national attention and sympathy.

Mr Zhou was from Henan province in central China, and on a visit to see the sights of Beijing he'd checked into a cheap hostel. It was near the central government's State Bureau for

Letters and Visits, where people lodge their complaints. Mr Zhou had the misfortune to be sharing his room with three people, also from Henan, who had travelled to the capital with a problem they wanted resolved, and one night without warning their room door was thrown open. Mr Zhou was dragged away with his three roommates and bundled into a van that set off back to Henan. Along the way he was beaten up and thrown from the vehicle. He was found unconscious by the side of the road. Chinese internet sites buzzed with indignation and six Henan officials were eventually punished. 'Perhaps the wrong person was caught,' said a spokesman. His statement was both true and unsettling. He seemed to imply that the mistake was in choosing the incorrect target: a tourist and not a complainant. The fact that a gang of thugs had carried out such a vile act in the first place was not the most important point of the story. Had Mr Zhou been visiting Beijing with an actual complaint, his assault would probably have gone unnoticed and unmentioned.

The story of the angry pensioners from Double River Farm had a postscript. The local authorities were well aware of the bad feeling, so took no chances when an important guest, a vice-mayor from Beijing, visited just a few days before the teacher and I were there. As the woman with the missing fingers told it, the dignitary had made the journey to unveil a new plaque outside the town's local government offices, proudly displaying the fact that this small enclave was still run by Beijing. But local officials were nervous. They were worried that residents might use the vice-mayor's visit to stage a demonstration, so they kept the trip a secret. When he came, the VIP unveiled the plaque and ate a quick lunch at the government-run guesthouse before heading quickly back to Qiqihar to spend the night. Most local people found out about the event only after it was over.

The teacher was intrigued and wanted to find out more.

He'd already spoken by telephone to the man in charge of propaganda in the town and the following morning he set off to find him. He walked over to the government offices, opposite our cheap hotel, taking along a bottle of rice wine as a gift. The teacher had a way of making people feel at ease, gently drawing out information that they initially might not want to give. I waited in the hotel room. I had wanted to go with him, but the teacher rightly pointed out that there would have been no chance of getting to the bottom of the story if I, a Western journalist, had gone along too. 'If you say "east", he'll say "west",' was how he put it.

About an hour later he was back with a grin on his face. The story was true. The vice-mayor had visited Double River Farm in the last few days and his stay had been kept a secret because the authorities feared locals might use it to stir up trouble. In public, officials from the highest to the lowest do not like to admit China is anything other than a stable, harmonious country, but under the surface there's often tension and dissatisfaction, and they know it.

I'd gone to Double River Farm to find out about the past, but so far I had only uncovered the present. The teacher promised me that at Ao'bao Mountain I would see something of what had gone on in the Cultural Revolution. Ao'bao Mountain is about 30 miles drive from Double River Farm. The teacher had been sent there about a month after that first journey to Heilongjiang. A group of youngsters from Company 56 were just settling into their new home in Double River Farm when they were told to march off again, to Ao'bao Mountain. They walked across snow-covered fields and the frozen Ah Lun River, one of the two waterways that give Double River Farm its name. The route was shorter than going by the road, but the freezing weather made it a difficult hike, and there was not much waiting for the youngsters when they got to their destination, just mud huts that served as dormitories. They were heated by *kangs*, stone beds with a fire underneath. These are still the only form of heating for many rural homes in northern China. At night it was too cold to sleep so the youngsters contemplated the sayings of Chairman Mao to keep each other going. At the time, the teacher still believed he and the other youngsters were carrying out a special mission for the Chairman.

Years after the Cultural Revolution, the teacher wrote a newspaper article about his time at Ao'bao Mountain. I'd read it and I recognised the area from his description as our car drew nearer. In truth, it's more hill than mountain, but in a district where the land is mostly flat I could see why the teacher had exaggerated. We were looking for a quarry, where the youngsters in 1969 had been forced to dig up stone. They'd used explosives to break up the rock, then carried the fragments to waiting carts. When they were not working they were forced to undergo military drills, using wooden guns, and sit through hours of political study sessions.

Wandering about the hill, it took us a long time to find the quarry. All the old buildings had gone and no one in the village next to the mountain had lived there in 1969, so they couldn't help us with what we were looking for. We were also slowed down by the teacher, whose high heels and tight trousers were unsuited to the terrain. It meant he could move only gingerly across the large blocks of stone, which looked as if they'd been thrown around by an angry giant. His friend, who was wearing more practical work boots, held the teacher's hand and guided him over the roughest patches. I looked back and watched them; they seemed such unlikely friends. The teacher was wearing pink sunglasses and matching lipstick. To complement his make-up he'd chosen a partially see-through pink T-shirt. A large handbag was slung over one shoulder. His friend was more suitably attired for the conditions. He'd put on a flat cap to keep out the wind and wore a thick jacket with matching trousers.

The friends had worked together in the Cultural Revolution, but their lives had followed different paths since then. That much was clear from their appearance. The teacher had gone back to the city and spent much of his working life in an office. He appeared uncomfortable in the countryside. At one point in our search for the quarry he'd stood on a muddy, rutted road in all his finery and asked directions from a man who was riding a cart pulled by two donkeys. In this poor, rural setting he couldn't have looked more out of place. But his friend was different. He'd stayed on in Double River Farm to work the land, something that was obvious from his thick forearms and blistered hands. There was a black patch on his left cheek, the result of frostbite from a particularly cold winter. We stumbled around for a while and eventually found what we were looking for: a quarry that is now no more than a big hole in the ground. It started to rain so we decided to leave; there wasn't much to look at anyway. The teacher had spent six hard and cold months on Ao'bao Mountain, a place that now exists only in his memory.

Or did it? From the teacher's collection of essays and articles, I searched for something that would give me a real sense of Ao'bao Mountain. It was clear that this wind-swept place was inhospitable, even in summer, but it must have been many times worse back then, when China was much poorer. What had the teacher felt? Finally, I came across a piece he'd written about one of the men who'd led Company 56, a platoon leader who'd been part of the welcome committee that met the teacher and his fellow teenagers when they'd first arrived in Heilongjiang. This frightening man usually wore a ferocious expression and had a habit of always trying to teach someone a lesson. In the article, the teacher describes

an incident that took place just after the youngsters had been
sent to Ao'bao Mountain to quarry stone.

Outside, snow that looked like goose feathers began to fall.
Inside, under the light of an oil lamp we dozen or so huddled at
the head of the kang and began to eat and talk about the turn
our lives had taken. Suddenly, the door was pushed open and
through the faint light of the lamp we saw the platoon leader
walk in. Why was he here? Had he come to tell us off? Each
of us stood to attention and waited to see what would happen
next. We wondered what disruption this leader had brought
to our door.

I began to feel what it must have been like for those terrified youngsters, little more than children, who'd been sent
away from the comfort of home to live as exiled prisoners.
History is full of people who've been forced to pack up and
move their lives, but had so many young people ever been
treated in such a callous manner? I thought perhaps not. I
went back to the teacher's article and read on.

'Come, let's pretend we're all old friends from Beijing,' said the
platoon leader, and from inside his coat he pulled out a bottle
of strong rice wine. He then took out a flask of hot water and
poured it into a basin. He put a little rice wine into a bowl
and then put the bowl into the basin, to warm the liquor. A
sweet fragrance began to fill the room. The platoon leader then
ordered us all to sit down. 'Today is your first day quarrying
stone. Let's drink a glass together.'

With pounding hearts, the teenagers wondered what was
going on, but they were too afraid not to do as they were
told.

No one had ever tasted rice wine before, least of all such a ferociously strong spirit as this. But under orders from the platoon
leader, we each opened our mouths and drained our cups. Was
it spicy? Was it sour? It felt like an electric current had shot
straight from my throat to my head. Then the platoon leader
opened his mouth and spoke. 'Everyone now knows the taste
of liquor. So far from your mothers and fathers in this great
northern wilderness, this moment marks the end to your days
as students. From now, you are all adults – and you will all act
like adults.'

Afterwards, the youngsters often asked the platoon leader
to drink with them again, but he would simply shake his
head and say: 'Not at the moment, let's wait for a better
opportunity.' It never came. He was ordered elsewhere and
the teacher never saw him again. But in subsequent years
whenever the teacher bumped into one of his comrades from
those days he would ask them if they'd heard anything of the
platoon leader. Without any real expectation of an answer,
he'd say: 'When do you think we'll get to have a drink with
him again?'

Back in Double River Farm there were other sites to visit
and other hardships to remember. The teacher took me to
what was once a brick factory, where the youngsters would
visit in secret in winter, to lay their coats on the kilns to warm
them. Of course, they often had to work there too. Another
back-breaking job involved digging up clods of earth, which
were then used to make a bank to stop the Ah Lun River
flooding the village. We also visited an old dormitory, from
where the teacher would set off in the early hours of the
morning to hoe and weed the fields until long after nightfall.
Food was always in short supply and the exiles were never
full. But as the teacher and his old friend reminisced over a
lunch that included several bottles of local beer, the hardships

seemed to increase. The two men engaged in a friendly battle to prove who had risen earliest, and before long they were both claiming to have got up just an hour or so after going to bed. It was hard to tell what was fact and what was fiction.

The teacher seemed to have taken a dislike to the woman with four stumps and the more he drank, the more he gave up trying to hide his feelings. He blamed her for the break-up of his friend's marriage and whenever she was not listening he kept referring to her as a 'worn out shoe', which in Chinese translates as 'loose woman'. Later on, we went to see his friend's former wife and their daughter. The two women were angry that the man in their lives had run off with a younger woman. Neither of them were at that point speaking to him. The teacher sympathised with them and while he told the daughter that it was her duty to speak to her father, he later had angry words with his friend. The teacher might wear unconventional clothes, but the incident revealed that he was a traditionalist when it came to marriage. 'I'd never divorce my wife. We've been together too long,' he said.

Despite the difficulties surrounding his friend's marital status, the teacher was enjoying himself. I found it difficult to understand why he was taking this pilgrimage to the past in his stride. After all, he'd arrived in Double River Farm when he was just eighteen and didn't leave until he was twenty-four. He'd missed critical years of his schooling and at that point had little hope of going to university or getting the kind of job he had dreamed about when he was a child. He had spent those years in the freezing north with little food and inadequate clothing, living in makeshift shelters. Most of the time he did hard, physical labour but, listening to the teacher chatting and drinking with his old friend, I could easily imagine they were talking about a very different past, one spent in the bosom of privilege. I suppose it was no different to the closeness and camaraderie experienced by other people in extreme situations. My grandad had used similar language to describe the friendships he made during the Second World War in Burma. 'We were all in it together,' said the teacher. 'We lived and worked and sang – and didn't have to worry about anything else.'

Something else struck me. Double River Farm has been shaped by the banishment of all those young people, but there was very little acknowledgement of this terrible episode. People would tell you their stories, just as the dumpling seller had, but there was no memorial or small museum where visitors might be reminded of the past. It's the same across China. People who went through the Cultural Revolution are mostly left to make sense of it by themselves. I'd heard before that former 'educated youths' had been making trips back to the places where they'd been sent as teenagers. Some of them found their way to Double River Farm. When the teacher went to find out about the visiting dignitary from Beijing, he'd also learned more about the town's government-run reception centre. It was built so those returning to have a look would have somewhere to eat and sleep. It was free. The fact that no one had to pay appeared to be a tacit admission that something bad had happened in the past, and the authorities in Double River Farm wanted, in a small way, to make amends.

The teacher had just one more task to fulfil before he left Heilongjiang. In those hard years at Double River Farm there had been little comfort, but one man had done his best to help: Wang Jiabao, the son of a landlord. The teacher's grandmother had been Jiabao's wet nurse in the 1930s and when her young charge grew up he kept in touch with her. During the Cultural Revolution he was living in Qiqihar. The teacher managed to visit this family friend on several occasions, to eat good food and get some rest, but he had not

seen his benefactor for almost 40 years and wanted to know if
he was still alive. In a bureaucratic country like China there's
a paper trail for everyone and the teacher was confident he
could track him down, even if he was dead, so we went back
to Qiqihar and began looking.

The teacher knew very little about Wang Jiabao, only that
he thought he'd once taught at the city's 1st Railway Middle
School, so that's where we started. In China, foreigners
are usually stopped from entering anywhere that might be
considered sensitive and most factories, schools and residen-
tial compounds have gates watched over by security guards.
But like anywhere in the world, confidence counts and the
teacher and I simply walked into the schoolyard as though
we were supposed to be there. Hundreds of teenage pupils
were jogging slowly around an exercise yard in blue and
white tracksuits that also served as their uniforms. Watched
over by a couple of bored teachers, they seemed to have
perfected the challenging task of running at a pace slightly
slower than walking.

The teacher and I went straight to the office block and
asked various people if they remembered Wang Jiabao. He
would have retired a long time ago, but Chinese workers
usually maintain ties with their former places of employment
so it wasn't unreasonable to think someone might remember
him. No one did, until we found an old man sorting through
files in a dusty office. He remembered Wang Jiabao, 'a big
man with a long face', but he thought the teacher's family
friend had taught at the 3rd Railway Middle School, not
the school we were in. We trudged back to an office where
we'd earlier spoken to a secretary and asked her to call the
correct school. A few minutes later she put the phone down
and turned, sombre faced, towards the teacher. 'I'm sorry,'
she said, 'but your friend died two years ago.' It was a disap-
pointing end to our journey. The teacher had not seen the

man who had helped him since 1972 and, after more than four decades, he'd arrived a couple of years too late. There was to be no tearful reunion.

At first, I didn't know what to say, thinking the teacher would be upset. But after a few moments he seemed to shrug off whatever disappointment he was feeling and stood up. 'At least we now have time to do something else,' he said, before marching out of the office, out of the school and back onto the streets of Qiqihar. The city's pavements were a patchwork of broken slabs, from where small-time traders sold fruit and vegetables or repaired bicycles. The shops that lined the main streets were as colourful as anywhere else in China, with giant writing advertising their products, but many had a careworn look about them. And behind the main streets were rows of scruffy apartment blocks, derelict buildings and smokestacks that no longer smoked. Nowadays, Chinese towns and cities usually feel like places where there's hope, where things are getting better, but I felt I'd never been anywhere as glum as Qiqihar.

The teacher hardly looked at his surroundings as he strode purposefully back to our hotel through the bustling streets. As we walked, he told me he wanted to change into a new outfit. When we'd visited the school, he'd been dressed as a man, presumably because the school authorities might not have helped if he'd been dressed as a woman. But now he wanted to make use of the last few hours we had in Qiqihar and get dressed up. The teacher changed quickly into a white dress decorated with pink flowers. It was short enough to reveal a considerable amount of thigh and was accompanied by high heels, a pearl necklace and a long black wig. He wanted to go to the park by the river and have some photographs taken, to remember our visit. As we came out of the hotel we passed the restaurant where we'd eaten the previous evening. The owner was standing in the doorway watching us pick our way carefully through the chaotic traffic. The teacher saw him and shouted: 'Do I look pretty?' He was showing off and didn't stop for the answer that the man was clearly struggling to put into words.

At the park we strolled around, admiring the trees and flowers. Despite the greenery, I often found these places depressing because there was usually something ugly to spoil the view. It could be a collection of ancient children's rides or an empty boating lake with litter strewn across the bottom, but there was usually something. The teacher though was making the best of it. He jumped on an empty swing, ignoring the quizzical looks from parents playing with their children. A few workers who'd come to the park to eat their lunch looked on with interest, as though they'd been presented with free entertainment that they weren't expecting. The teacher handed me his camera and asked me to stand in front of him and take some photographs. 'How do I look?' he asked, as he swung backwards and forwards. It wasn't the most comfortable task I'd ever been given and I stood awkwardly trying to focus the camera as he went to and fro, kicking his feet high into the air and revealing un-asked-for glimpses of what lay beneath. I clicked away as his dress flapped in the breeze. Later over lunch he studied the pictures carefully and was pleased with how they'd come out.

How A Food Flavouring
Changed The Teacher's Life

During our trip to Double River Farm the teacher alternated
between men's and women's clothing, depending on how he
felt and what the circumstances required. When he visited
the town's propaganda chief, to find out about the visiting
Beijing dignitary who'd been reluctant to hang around, he
dressed as a man. That seemed logical. He wanted information, not questions about his choice of clothing. But when
we were by ourselves or meeting friends he preferred female
clothing. Our visit to Double River Farm came a few weeks
after he'd first revealed his other self to me and he seemed
keen to dress as a woman whenever he could. The inside of
his suitcase revealed the thought he'd put into how he would
look on the trip. He showed me a range of cosmetics that
he'd neatly lined up on the window ledge of his hotel room.
He'd also brought along several pairs of shoes, a couple of
wigs and countless other delicate items of female clothing.

The teacher didn't just keep changing his clothes: he
would also alter his mood and his mannerisms along with his
outfit. His frame of mind seemed to depend on what he was
wearing. Clothed as a man, he would be his usual self: slightly
cynical, witty and in no mood to accept any nonsense, but as
a woman he was far softer. He would occasionally toss his
head from side to side and when he walked he would sway
his hips like a model on a catwalk. That feminine walk did

not always come off. He said he felt more comfortable in high heels than in men's flat shoes, but his unsteady progress in women's footwear made me suspect that he was not being entirely honest.

It's not always easy for foreigners to form real, deep friendships with Chinese people. I found most locals unfailingly polite and willing to show hospitality to people they barely knew, but many find it hard to fully open up to a foreigner. That's no doubt the result of years of propaganda from the Chinese government, which suggests that people from overseas don't really understand China and should be treated with caution. There's also a language barrier that prevents the development of many relationships. So I was pleased to be finding out so much about the teacher and grateful that he was willing to confide in me. But his cross-dressing did present me with a problem.

We were travelling to various points across China in order to write his story. I wanted to see how China had changed and how he'd changed with it. The women's clothes were obviously a big part of his life, but from the moment he told me about his semi-secret existence I suspected he'd want to keep it that way. How was I going to write a book about a journey through China with a Chinese pensioner wearing women's clothes without being able to mention the clothes? I decided to tackle the question head on, so on that first evening in Changsha when he told me about his cross-dressing I asked him if I could write about what he was wearing in the book. 'I'll think about it,' he said.

We left the question hanging for several weeks. It wasn't until we were travelling by train to Qiqihar that I plucked up enough courage to broach the subject again. I was afraid he'd say no, leaving me with no option but to abandon the whole project. But I had to know the answer, so when we settled down into our bunks after a pleasant dinner in the dining car

I asked him again if I could mention his choice of clothing in the book. He said no. He was worried that because of the internet his story, even if it was initially written in English, would find its way back to China, and would probably be translated into Chinese. Everyone would know his story. He told me that his wife knew about his cross-dressing, but didn't really approve. He didn't want to cause her any embarrassment. I was disappointed and a little cross. Why hadn't he just told me before we embarked on our scheme? We could have cancelled the book before we'd even begun researching it. I dropped the subject, picked up a newspaper and pretended to read, but really I sat there silently thinking some unpleasant thoughts.

In Double River Farm, I tried talking to him again about the difficulty of not mentioning what he was wearing. I explained that I would probably have to drop the project because it would simply not be honest enough. I asked him to imagine what it would be like to write about a journey across China with someone who was black – and not mention the person's colour. Apart from a few foreigners who live in a handful of cities, China has no black people so they usually draw crowds or comments. To my surprise, the teacher seemed to take in what I was saying and suddenly agreed that what he wore on our travels could become part of the story, as long as I didn't reveal his name. It was a deal and in order not to jeopardise it, or give him the opportunity to change his mind, I didn't mention the subject again.

Later, I was a little disappointed with myself for reacting angrily to the teacher's misgivings. After all, he was in a difficult position. He wasn't deliberately trying to under-mine the story I was writing, he was simply worried about what people, particularly his family, might think about his cross-dressing if his story became public knowledge. He was right to be concerned, as a report sponsored by the United

Nations in 2016 made clear. It explored attitudes towards sexual and gender minorities in China and came to a series of sobering conclusions. It found that almost no one among these two groups was willing to reveal their true selves to school friends or work colleagues. Only one in 20 was brave enough to come out. A few more were honest with their families, but not many more. Like most countries, China is still adapting to the idea that a person's sexual orientation or gender expression can take different forms. Prejudice and discrimination remain commonplace. On top of that, the teacher was in a particularly vulnerable position because his cross-dressing made him extremely visible. A gay man can remain anonymous in public if he wants, but when the teacher dressed as a woman he left no one in any doubt that he was a man dressed as a woman.

I'd also perhaps underplayed the pull of family ties. They're obviously important everywhere, but the traditions, conventions and duties surrounding this social unit appear so much stronger in China. By contrast, the individual is of little importance. Sometimes I'd convince myself that Chinese society contains only two really critical institutions: the state and the family. There's nothing much in between. In Chinese families, children are of primary importance. Confucian tradition demands that there are descendants to carry on the family name; not to provide them is considered the worst kind of unfilial conduct. That's why many gay people in China – even today – are forced into heterosexual relationships that will result in children. The teacher is not gay, he just enjoys wearing women's clothes, but I could see how his cross-dressing might not fit in with how he viewed his obligations towards his family.

The UN survey into people's attitudes towards those who don't conform to society's norms was not all bad reading. It suggested a country in transition, where people are ever more open about what they are willing to accept. It seems a growing number of Chinese citizens are increasingly relaxed about issues surrounding sex. A majority now believe in equal rights for sexual and gender minorities. This matched my own experiences with the teacher during our travels across China. I never once saw a negative reaction to what he was wearing. People would sometimes be amused or keen to ask a question, but no one was openly scornful. And there was never any hint of violence. Even in the West, where attitudes on this issue are usually more enlightened, there's always the possibility that a cross-dresser will arouse anger. But it was something I never encountered with the teacher. Chinese people's traditional reputation for gentleness is well founded.

These reflections came only later. As our train pulled out of Qiqihar I was simply relieved that the visit had gone well and I could write about the teacher's clothing. Double River Farm had been a pivotal place in the teacher's early life and I was pleased we'd decided to go there. As a general rule, going and seeing something for yourself is always a good idea, particularly in China. When I'd first started working for the BBC in Beijing I used to spend many hours in the office on the telephone trying to track down officials, in order to confirm a piece of news or set up an interview. I would invariably fail. The official would be out, the information would not be to hand or – and this happened all the time – no one would even bother to pick up the phone.

From this experience it would have been easy to conclude that nothing much of importance was going on anywhere in the country. That was clearly not the case. The answer was always to go and have a look, because only then would the full colour and richness of life in China reveal itself. That's why I'd been so keen for the teacher to show me his life as well as tell me his story. As I looked across to the next bunk,

I could see the teacher was also happy with how things had gone. He'd revisited a former place of exile and found out what had happened to Wang Jiabao, the family friend. As our evening train chugged away from that grim northern city, its gentle rocking motion lulled us into a peaceful and contented sleep.

For the return journey we'd decided to buy standard-class sleeper tickets and had beds that faced each other. A standard sleeping car in China is a little like camping on iron wheels. Compartments have no doors and are separated from each other by a partition wall. Each compartment has six bunk beds, three on either side. The teacher and I were in the two middle bunks. Beds are packed so tightly that you can reach out and touch the person opposite. In the morning I woke up to see the teacher, just a few feet away, laid on his back with his hands behind his head, staring at the underside of the bunk above him. He was in a talkative mood so we began chatting. The carriage below us was a hive of activity; people were pulling on clothes or disappearing to brush their teeth. Some slurped tea out of what looked like jam jars, while others ate their breakfast at tiny tables just below the window of each compartment.

The teacher began telling me about a trip he'd organised while working for the propaganda department of a Beijing food company in the early 1990s, a part of his life we hadn't yet explored. One of his bosses had wanted to visit a factory just outside the capital, so the teacher had gathered together a fleet of company cars to take him and his staff there. They'd set off and were nearly at their destination when suddenly they came to a halt and the boss got out. He had a problem. He was being driven in the lead car, an expensive Japanese four-wheel-drive that he didn't want to be seen in. The Chinese Communist Party regularly launches campaigns against corruption and at the time no official was supposed to have a car that didn't match their rank. The boss was worried that his vehicle looked too good and someone might report him. To appear as humble as possible, he got out of his car and went to sit in a far more modest Volkswagen Santana towards the back of the convoy. It's a mode of transport that was at one time a favourite with a certain level of official. The teacher had originally been in the Santana and so he went and sat in the expensive Japanese car at the front. The convoy then set off again.

All seemed well, but unfortunately no one at the factory knew what the boss looked like or in which car he would be travelling. When they pulled up the waiting delegation naturally assumed that the main man would be sitting in the expensive vehicle at the front. They rushed to open the door and bowed as the teacher, looking embarrassed and stumbling for words, stepped out. He quickly regained his composure and explained to the waiting delegation that they'd made a mistake, at which point the welcome party dashed off to greet the real boss, who was by this time standing impatiently next to the scruffy car at the back of the convoy. It was the kind of comic misunderstanding the teacher loved to talk about. Class distinctions were supposed to have been abolished in China, but in reality people are finely attuned to even the slightest difference in wealth and rank.

The story had taken a long time to tell because the teacher would occasionally break out into fits of laughter, which became more frequent as he moved towards the conclusion of his tale. When the teacher laughed his whole body shook, an action that began to reveal a previously unseen aspect of his attire. He'd slept in the clothes he'd worn the previous day when we left Qiqihar: a tight T-shirt and what looked like a padded bra beneath. As he laughed, a piece of skin-coloured plastic started to push up out of the top of his

T-shirt. I had no idea what it was and was a little wary of asking, so said nothing. The piece of plastic continued to work itself loose from the teacher's clothing until, at one particularly funny moment in his story, it jumped clean out of his T-shirt and fell down onto the head of the man below, who was bent over a bowl of steaming noodles. The teacher instantly swooped down from his bunk and scooped up the piece of plastic, which I could now see was a fake breast, complete with tiny nipple. He quickly stuffed it back into his bra and carried on with his story as if nothing had happened. It was all so quick that the man eating the noodles didn't know what had hit him.

The teacher's journey from Qiqihar back to Beijing in the 1970s had not been anywhere near as easy as the one we took together, and there certainly hadn't been any incidents involving plastic breasts. When he finally moved home the Cultural Revolution was on the wane, but it hadn't yet been abandoned. The chaos did not simply end overnight; it faded away over a period of years. As the initial revolutionary enthusiasm died away, many who'd been persecuted were quietly rehabilitated. Deng Xiaoping, the leader who would eventually introduce economic reforms and open up China to the rest of the world, went back to running the country. For much of the Cultural Revolution he'd been working in a tractor repair factory, a task he'd been given when he fell out with Mao. Deng was purged a second time in 1976, but that was just a few months before the Chairman's death and he managed to get back into politics again.

Some of the young people who'd been ordered out of the cities to work in the countryside began to drift back home too. It would take some of them many years to be officially allowed to return, by which time much of their youth and enthusiasm had vanished. The teacher started the process of leaving Double River Farm by spending longer and longer periods in Beijing when he returned to the capital each summer. There was still work to be done in the countryside, but the teacher didn't fancy doing it so visits to his parents that were supposed to last just a week or so stretched on for months. At the end of 1975 he managed to persuade a sympathetic doctor in Heilongjiang that a stomach ache was a serious illness. The doctor wrote him a sick note that allowed him to miss work. That note was then sent to the authorities in Beijing and two months later they agreed to let him return home for good. 'I cheated them, but they knew they were being cheated,' said the teacher. 'They didn't mind. They deliberately turned a blind eye.'

For the teacher, the Cultural Revolution was over, but his troubles had not yet ended. He was already twenty-four and had missed out on an education. He had no qualifications. They would have been useless anyway because Chairman Mao was still alive and no one dared dismantle the system he'd put in place. At the time, it was better to be 'red' than 'expert'; an individual's political outlook mattered more than the ability to actually do a job well. Most people were still at least outwardly loyal to this ideal. The teacher was offered a job as a sales assistant in a food shop, but he refused to do it. For a young man who dreamed of meaningful work it was impossible to rouse himself to such a task. He spent the next two years at home in the Alley of One Hundred Children doing very little before being offered another job working in a soy sauce factory. By then boredom made any kind of work seem attractive, so he took it. It was a wise decision because the job proved to be a turning point. Rarely in the annals of human history can a food flavouring have offered a way out of drudgery, but that's how it turned out for the teacher.

As well as producing a famous brand of soy sauce the factory also cooked up monosodium glutamate (MSG), and that's where the teacher was assigned. The plant ran to a familiar rhythm, irrespective of the political changes taking place outside the factory gates. China was beginning to awake from the torpor of the Cultural Revolution, but the workers inside the soy sauce plant had to continue making the country's favourite food flavourings. There were three shifts: morning, afternoon and night. To keep the workers cool in summer heat not yet made bearable by air conditioning, they wore beige uniforms made from silk. In winter they were given blue padded clothes to keep out the cold. The teacher mostly cycled to work, which was on the other side of the city, along streets that in those days rarely saw a car.

Making MSG is monotonous work. The teacher's job was to monitor the changing chemical composition of the ingredients, which were mixed together in a large vat. His most important task was to make sure the balance between the solution's acid and alkaline content was just right. He would stare for hours at a gauge that registered each tiny change. 'It wasn't hard work, but it was tiring,' said the teacher. 'Sometimes on a night shift I would fall asleep and get the mixture wrong. It would all have to be thrown away.' For several years the teacher worked through this dull routine, fermenting the small white MSG crystals that give a kick to savoury food, while secretly dreaming of escape. And then somewhere in those long hours of toil sprang an idea. The teacher had often thought of becoming a writer, but what could he write about? He decided to follow the age-old adage that it's best to stick to a familiar topic, so chose a subject that was all around him: MSG.

Of all the world's flavour enhancers, MSG has perhaps the greatest potential to produce an interesting story. It was invented in 1908 by a Japanese professor, Kikunae Ikeda, who wanted to isolate the delicious taste he'd detected in his favourite seaweed broth. The flavour was neither sweet nor sour, bitter or salty. Professor Ikeda called it 'umami'. He was able to extract glutamate from the soup and realised that it was this substance that had provided the pleasant savoury taste. He patented his discovery and opened up a whole new chapter in the history of food flavouring. There were now five tastes instead of just four. MSG found particular favour with chefs in China, Japan and Korea, although for some diners it has a rather unsavoury reputation. As the teacher slogged away on the production line, an argument was raging elsewhere in the world about the safety of MSG.

The row was ignited in 1968 by the Chinese-American researcher Dr Robert Ho Man Kwok, who wrote an article for the *New England Journal of Medicine* that detailed symptoms he experienced about 20 minutes after eating northern Chinese food. He described numbness in the back of his neck, general weakness and palpitations. After the article appeared, other people began to write to the journal describing similar symptoms and soon there was an intense and angry public debate about MSG. Several governments launched investigations to find out if there was any scientific basis to this distrust of monosodium glutamate. One organisation that became involved was the US Food and Drug Administration, which eventually asked a panel of experts to look into what had by then become known as 'Chinese restaurant syndrome'. It concluded that MSG was safe, just as other scientists have done, but suspicions about the food flavouring have lingered on and there are still people who insist on having no MSG in their favourite Chinese food.

Interestingly, it's occasionally suggested that the dislike of MSG, despite all the evidence that it does no harm, is essentially a racist reaction that stems from a general prejudice against China. It's easy to see how some Westerners might view the kitchens of Chinese restaurants, with their noise and dirt and unusual cooking techniques, as something to be wary of. And it's only a small journey from 'wary' to 'distrust' to 'blame' if a diner happens to fall ill after a meal. The name 'Chinese restaurant syndrome' is also unhelpful. In the minds of some, it will have only added to the sense that Chinese chefs are up to no good in the kitchen. It pins the blame for the migraines and aches and tiredness quite clearly on the Chinese. Another explanation for the distrust of monosodium glutamate might be found in its slightly scary acronym. MSG sounds like what it is: a chemical compound. In an age when people are more conscious than ever about what they put into their mouths, few people enjoy the thought of ingesting chemicals. Campaigners looking to persuade people to consume less salt would probably have more success if they called this staple food enhancer by its other name: sodium chloride.

Despite living in a China that was largely closed off from the rest of the world, the teacher was aware of the controversy surrounding MSG and alluded to the suspicions about the food flavouring in his article. But this first step towards a career with words largely stuck to the facts of how MSG is produced and the benefits it can bring. He praised its ability to improve brain function and mentioned its value for people with elevated levels of ammonia in their blood. In the end, he dismissed the worries about MSG with a last paragraph that was perhaps a little gullible, bearing in mind the countless food scandals that have emerged in China over recent years:

> Finally, let's talk about the dangers of MSG in food. The majority of MSG production in our country uses a starch hydrolysis fermentation process. Each part of the production line has a proper quality inspection system. National rules limit the amount of arsenic, iron, lead, zinc and other properties in MSG. You could say that the production of MSG in this country is fully in line with human needs.

It was a short article of no more than a few hundred Chinese characters and would struggle to interest the casual reader. Looking back, even the teacher admits it was not the most inspiring place to start a career with words. But it was a start. The article was published in a science journal and his boss was pleased. The teacher was at the time classified as just an ordinary worker, but he'd shown that his skills were perhaps not best employed on the production line. His ability with language would eventually allow him to escape the factory.

The teacher is not the only Chinese person for whom words were important. Listening to him tell his story about his association with MSG reminded me of when I'd met Zhou Youguang, the man who became known as the father of Pinyin. Pinyin is a writing system that allows Chinese characters to be written in the Roman alphabet, making it easier for beginners to learn to pronounce the thousands of sometimes extremely complex symbols that make up the Chinese written script. Hundreds of millions of Chinese schoolchildren, and countless foreigners who've grappled with the language, owe a debt of gratitude to Zhou Youguang. The system he helped devise in the 1950s has made learning Chinese much easier. After his great achievement, Mr Zhou went on to write dozens of books and when I met him, long after his 100th birthday, he could look back on a life full of words. At one time those words had saved him from political persecution, but by the time I met him they had made him something of an outcast in the China he had done so much to help.

Words had saved Zhou Youguang while he was still on the Pinyin project. When the communist party took power in China in 1949 he was working as a banker on Wall Street in New York. Like many other Chinese people living abroad at that time, he decided to return home in the belief that he could help forge a new nation. These returning expatriates trusted Chairman Mao when he said he wanted to build a new democracy. Mr Zhou initially worked as an economics teacher at Shanghai's prestigious Fudan University, but was then asked to become the head of a committee whose task was to devise a new system of Romanising the Chinese language. At first he resisted, arguing that he had no experience in this field, but then a friend persuaded him to take the job.

For decades, Chinese leaders had wanted to make it easier for their mostly illiterate people to learn to read and write. Other systems had already been developed, but none had proved durable enough to stop the search for something more suitable. Mr Zhou and his committee took three years to render Chinese into the Latin script. People at the time laughed at how long it had taken. 'Three years for just 26 letters, they would joke,' said Mr Zhou, who laughed as he remembered the gentle criticism he and his team had to endure. It took many more years for Pinyin to become the internationally accepted system of Romanising Chinese characters, but Mr Zhou and his colleagues had achieved something that others had only dreamed about.

As Zhou Youguang and his committee struggled in the world of letters, China was changing. The communists had initially welcomed all kinds of people and all shades of opinion in order to get the country moving after decades of war and strife. But that changed when in 1957 Mao launched his first big national campaign to push the country further to the left. The Anti-Rightist Movement was aimed at weeding out intellectuals who were, in Mao's view, too far to the right of the political spectrum. A year earlier the Chairman had launched the colourfully named Hundred Flowers Campaign, which urged people to give their views on how the new regime was doing. Thousands spoke out, with many revealing their animosity towards China's new government.

Mao quickly backtracked and launched the Anti-Rightist Movement, which persecuted those who he'd originally encouraged to speak out. Many of those accused were sent to re-education camps, where they wasted years on menial tasks, work many of them would repeat during the Cultural Revolution a decade later. Afterwards, Mao claimed that he'd planned the two campaigns from the beginning: the first to entice the snakes out of their caves, the second to cut them down after they had revealed themselves. But perhaps the truth is that Mao was taken aback by the torrent of criticism his government faced during the Hundred Flowers Campaign, forcing him to silence those who had been foolish enough to speak their minds.

For people caught up in the Anti-Rightist Movement, it was sometimes a matter of life and death. Those who had returned to China from abroad were obvious targets because they were tainted with the capitalist world in which many had once lived. Many of Mr Zhou's friends and former students committed suicide or were forced out of their jobs. Mr Zhou believes he was saved only because of the work he was doing with the language committee.

When I interviewed Zhou Youguang he was living in a shabby apartment block in central Beijing. His wife had also enjoyed a long life, but she'd died a few years before and so Mr Zhou was on his own, helped only by a maid who doubled up as an assistant. His flat was sparsely furnished and had little in the way of decoration: many of the walls were bare concrete. It looked like no one had touched them since the building had been first put up. Mr Zhou occupied a chair next to a big window, where light streamed in onto books and papers that were piled up around him. The surroundings seemed too spartan for a man who had helped millions of people read and write, and I couldn't help thinking that surely he deserved something better. Mr Zhou explained that his views had made him unpopular with the ruling communist party. He was not what you would call a dissident and at such an advanced age it was hard to see him as a threat. After all, he could hardly walk. But the party doesn't like anyone who speaks their mind without regard for its opinions. People like Mr Zhou are simply too individualistic to fit into a collectivist system. His books are filled with forthright opinions distilled from a lifetime of experiences and are not the kind of thing encouraged by the party, which wants the sole right to define everything from God to the price of pork. I asked Mr Zhou if he was afraid he would get in trouble with the police for being so open in our interview. Not for the first time in our conversation he laughed. 'What are they going to do, come and take me away?'

Mr Zhou lived a long life. He was one hundred and eleven when he died, and when I spoke to him I couldn't help but feel a little overawed. He'd done and seen so much, and all those experiences had shaped his thinking. At one point I asked a question that I thought offered a new and fresh perspective on life. But before I'd finished speaking he raised his hand to stop me, then pressed a buzzer that called his assistant. 'Get me the book on so and so,' he asked her. The assistant went away and came back a few minutes later carrying a publication from Mr Zhou's extensive back catalogue. They must have been stacked up in another room. 'This might answer your question,' he said handing over the book. It happened twice more. I would be mid-way through a question when Mr Zhou would call his assistant and get her to fetch me a book that would explain what I wanted to know. In the nicest way possible, I felt humbled. Mr Zhou had long ago thought of questions that I was only just beginning to form. He'd not only answered those questions, he'd written books about them.

As I've said, Mr Zhou laughed a lot during our meeting and

I wondered why he was so cheerful. When the communists came to power he'd been living an interesting and comfortable life in America, and didn't need to return to China. You could say he'd been tricked into coming home; lured by promises that never materialised. China under Mao did not develop as Mr Zhou had hoped. So why wasn't he angry? Mr Zhou's personal life had also contained many hardships and disappointments. During the Cultural Revolution he'd been sent to Ningxia in western China, where he spent many pointless years. He'd also experienced personal tragedies of the kind that many families went through during China's chaotic twentieth century. After our interview as I was flicking through a book written by Mr Zhou and his wife, I came across one particularly moving passage. It described an incident in May 1941 when the devoted couple were living in Sichuan province, in south-western China, with their two young children: Xiaoping, their son, and Xiaohe, their daughter. The piece was written by Zhou Youguang's wife:

Youguang was again not at home. One day Xiao He said she had a stomach ache. I thought she'd eaten something that wasn't clean, but very quickly she developed a fever. I was a little scared. We were living in the countryside at the time and the war was on; there were no doctors and no medicine. After three days she hadn't improved in the slightest and I realised it couldn't go on like this. I had to find someone to help me take my daughter to hospital in Chongqing. The doctor there said it was appendicitis and because we hadn't come earlier it had already begun to fester. After two months the doctor was no longer able to keep our baby girl alive. In July, just before her sixth birthday, she died. My tears ran dry. For more than half a century, I haven't been able to speak of this terrible incident to anyone. As for Xiao Ping, I put all my love onto his shoulders.

Zhou Youguang's optimism was something I'd often encountered in China. People seem able to endure years of hardship and disappointment without giving up. I would occasionally ask what made them carry on. They would invariably shrug their shoulders and utter one of the most commonly used phrases in the Chinese language: *mei banfa*, which broadly translates as, there's nothing that can be done; things are as they are. The phrase also seems to suggest a deeper patience, which comes from a realisation that not everything in life is possible. In China I'd often had cause to stop and admire this ability to accept the unacceptable. I realised early on that this is one of the reasons the communists have been able to stay in power for so long, despite introducing a series of catastrophic policies that have resulted in millions of deaths. People are simply too used to shrugging their shoulders and getting on with life.

I found it hard to escape the conclusion that Chinese people seem almost pre-conditioned to endure a dictatorial government, far more than most others. I asked Mr Zhou why, despite his difficulties, he always seemed to be laughing. He gave an indulgent smile, as if he was about to explain to a callow youth something that was self-evident to anyone with just a little wisdom. 'Everything has a good and a bad side,' he said. 'Besides, I'm a pragmatist: what's the point of regretting?' It's an argument that's difficult to refute.

This passivity shouldn't always be seen as a bad thing. It was born of a desire to get on with the important tasks in life and not get bogged down with things that don't matter. One story that illustrates this point involves the eighteenth-century Emperor Qianlong. It's said the emperor once visited southern China and saw a vast fleet of ships sailing to and fro on the ocean. He asked a minister accompanying him what all those people on all those hundreds of vessels were doing. The minister apparently replied that he saw only two ships and their names were 'fame' and 'wealth'. In China, there's a long-standing belief that attending to what some might consider the small things in life – home, family, garden – is more important than chasing dreams that don't really matter, like building a business or changing the world. The minister was articulating that thought. He believed the people on those ships were wasting their time on what would eventually prove to be unnecessary and unfulfilling tasks.

There's another story that takes the idea a little further. It suggests that of those twin goals – fame and wealth – the former is the hardest to shake off. Many people have been able to turn their backs on money, but fewer have been able to resist the lure of being adored. The story involves a conversation between a monk and his pupil. 'It's easier to get rid of the desire for money than to get rid of the desire for fame,' said the monk. 'Even retired scholars and monks still want to be distinguished and well known among their company. They want to give public discourses to a large audience and not retire to a small monastery talking to one pupil, like you and me now.' The pupil replied: 'Indeed, master, you are the only man in the world who has conquered the desire for fame.' The monk simply gave a knowing smile.

Perhaps Mr Zhou was happy because during his long life he'd realised that words that reflect the truth invariably outlast lies. In China it's not always easy to work out which is which, something that I'd encountered many times as a reporter. The Chinese government often accuses foreign correspondents of turning black into white and distorting the truth but, to my ears, the language of its spokespeople proves the point that words and meaning can sometimes part company. This is most obviously on show at the regular briefings given to the media by China's foreign ministry. It's the main channel by which the government explains itself to the rest of the world. Most overseas journalists in China spend at least some time going to these briefings, and many marvel at how its spokespeople keep a straight face as they give voice to a predictable and constantly repeated list of platitudes, half-truths and misleading statements.

The case of the Chinese lawyer Gao Zhisheng is a perfect illustration. He was once lauded by the Chinese authorities, but then persecuted when he started representing people who disagreed with the government. He was put in prison and released, a process that happened several times. During one of his brief periods on the outside he claimed he'd been tortured. When he was released for the last time his broken spirit appeared to confirm his allegations of abuse. The once-confident and boastful Gao Zhisheng seemed cowed and diminished. Understandably, the foreign ministry fended off many questions about the lawyer and one particular answer sticks in my mind as a perfect example of the strange statements Chinese officials sometimes find themselves uttering. At the time of the question, Mr Gao had just disappeared, presumably once again into the arms of China's internal security apparatus. Foreign journalists wanted to know where he was. 'He's where he should be,' was the baffling reply. It might have been true, after all, everyone is always somewhere, and communist party officials might have truly believed they'd put him in the right place. But it was an evasive answer that raised more than a few disturbing questions.

It's this kind of public statement, intended to obscure the truth, that has allowed ridiculous rumours to gain such high value in China. People are often more willing to believe a fantastical story they think *might* be true, rather than an official announcement that they know will be, at best, only *partially* true. The government tries hard to suppress these rumours, censoring the media and the thoughts of individuals expressed in online postings. Officials know that an alternative reading of current events might undermine their own carefully constructed explanation of reality. And those who go further, by suggesting other ways in which Chinese people might live, face even harsher punishments. The Nobel Peace Prize winner Liu Xiaobo was hardly suggesting revolution when he helped draft a document called Charter '08. It asked Chinese people to reject the idea of an 'enlightened overlord' and instead turn towards a system of liberties, democracy and the rule of law. The communist party itself debates such questions internally, but it's a different matter when someone outside the party discusses these issues. Liu Xiaobo was sentenced to 11 years in prison.

So, words in China can get you into trouble and can even get you sent to prison. Often you have to be very brave, or so old that you no longer care about the consequences, to write what you want. Fortunately for the teacher, his first article about MSG did not warrant attention from the censors. But it did prove to be a pivotal moment in his life. It gave him the confidence to think and write. In subsequent years he wrote about the tree that once stood in the centre of his courtyard home and about his tough upbringing on Ao'bao Mountain. He even wrote about simple, life-changing events, such as getting a telephone installed for the first time. That first article about MSG gave him the strength to believe he would someday be able to find a better job, one more suited to his abilities and interests. But before he could move on to something better, he had to get himself the education he had missed as a teenager.

A Few Lessons On Governing

The teacher seemed to have an anecdote to fit every situation. If there was something troubling me he would invariably draw on his experiences to help me understand. By doing this, he was displaying a characteristic I'd slowly come to notice and admire in many Chinese people: their ability to learn from life. In China, this useful tool has been turned into an art form, and it's not just individuals who learn from their own life. Wisdom acquired over centuries of unbroken civilisation has been distilled into pithy sayings known as *chengyu*. These are short morality tales reduced to just a few Chinese characters to help people navigate everyday problems. They pepper people's conversations and the teacher would often use them. These sayings reveal a willingness by Chinese people to adapt to the realities of life; to seek the best wherever the best can be found. I'm paying the teacher a compliment when I say that he didn't seem to believe in anything, no religion and no moral code, unless it could be shown to help him live a better life. Like generations of Chinese people before him, he is a practical man unconcerned with ideas that have little benefit to everyday life.

There's a wonderful example of this attitude in the work of Lin Yutang, a Chinese author writing in the first half of the twentieth century. His books introduced China and its people to a global audience. In one, called *My Country and My People*, he explains the Chinese approach to life by quoting Confucius. When asked by one of his disciples to give his thoughts on death and the afterlife, the philosopher's answer was short and straight to the point. Rendered by Lin Yutang into pidgin English, Confucius told his follower: 'Don't know life – how know death?' The comment reveals little about what happens when we die, but a great deal about the here and now. Confucius was acknowledging the difficulty of getting through life and finding the best way to live. He was focusing all his energy on this world, instead of a later one that might or might not exist. As Lin Yutang put it, Confucius had a practical attitude towards the problems of life. It was an outlook the teacher would often employ to help me understand any knotty issue, and it explains why he remained so calm in the face of events that made my blood boil.

One day I was struggling with a difficulty that I've never really solved: how is China governed? In the BBC office in Beijing we had a wall chart that showed each government department and how they relate to one another. Photographs of the various ministers were placed above the departments they controlled. We also had another chart that showed the different bureaux of the Chinese Communist Party, which has ruled China without pause since 1949. The second chart contained many of the same faces as the first, but this time they had different jobs: a government minister on one might appear as a senior party official on the other. The problem, never made clear on either of the charts, was to understand how the communist party is linked to the government, which is in charge, and how orders are transmitted from one to the other. As usual, the teacher was willing to help.

His essential point was to disregard the wall charts because in China official titles and procedures are always less important than the people behind them, a lesson he had learned at the soy sauce factory when he'd taken part in an election. It had been arranged to choose a representative for the workers who toiled on the MSG production line. There were about 100 people on the workshop floor and all of them voted. The teacher won with 60 votes, receiving about twice as many as his nearest rival, but his victory was short lived. The next day his manager told him that the person who'd come second would get the job. 'Don't make a fuss, it'll only turn out badly,' the teacher was told. Apparently, the losing candidate had better connections with the factory bosses and so they gave him the position, regardless of the election result.

The role of connections, or *guanxi*, is a powerful force in China. Good connections sometimes matter more than money, more than rank and occasionally more than common sense. That's the way it's been for centuries and after the teacher told me his election story he shrugged his shoulders. As a practical man, he'd listened to his manager, worked out there was nothing he could do to change the situation and simply accepted the outcome. *Mei banfa*, he said, once again giving voice to that popular phrase.

Like many people I met in China, the teacher didn't seem very interested in politics. He had an intrinsic feel for how the system worked, but it wasn't something he could do much about, so he mostly ignored it. Life was going well so why bother rocking the boat? But I was fascinated by the subject and decided early on in my time in China that the only way to understand what was going on was to talk to as many people as possible. That's how I met Li Jianjun, the head of the local government in Yongning county in Ningxia, an arid region in the west of China that has a large population of Muslims. He was the first Chinese politician I'd managed to get close to. Chinese officials, particularly junior ones, are often reluctant to meet foreign journalists for fear of saying something wrong or, even worse, something revealing. It had taken us months to get permission to spend a day with Mr Li and in the end it was possible only because a Chinese producer at the BBC in Beijing knew someone who worked in the regional government in Ningxia. That was *guanxi* at work again. I didn't mind because it was a rare opportunity to get close to someone who had power, even if it was in just one small county. On the day we were supposed to visit, Mr Li had a busy schedule, so busy in fact that he tried to cancel at the last minute, citing his heavy workload. But I wanted to see him working hard and making decisions while under pressure. I was more determined than ever to spend a day with him and we managed to brush aside his objections.

The first item on the day's agenda was a meeting for 200 or so officials at the local government headquarters to discuss a new irrigation project. It was the type of meeting that communist countries seem to specialise in: very long and very dull. Two speakers, Mr Li and the county's communist party boss, droned on for three and a half hours. I sat at the back trying to understand their cumbersome official language. They seemed to be using so many words to say so little. Members of the audience drifted off; some even slept with their heads slightly bowed. It made them look as if they were staring intently at the notes they held in front of them. Apart from the speeches, the only other sound came from a tea lady as she walked up and down the aisles refilling everyone's cup. Chinese tea cups usually come with a lid so there was a little rattle every time someone received a fresh brew. The good thing about nodding off in the middle of an official speech in China is that there are always clues as to when the end is near. Officials usually speed up as they draw towards their conclusion and their voices go up in pitch, so the audience knew just when to clap. When Mr Li and the party boss had finally finished, a rumble of applause went round the room and everyone jumped up and walked out as fast as seemed polite. They reminded me of a class of bored schoolchildren who'd suddenly heard the bell that signalled the start of the summer holidays.

Mr Li declared himself satisfied with the meeting. 'We've achieved our aims, unified our thinking and defined our tasks,' he said, as he rushed back to his office, where he swapped his Western-style business jacket for a military-look camouflage coat. He'd changed because we were off to another function connected with the irrigation project that we'd just spent several hours hearing about, and at this next event he might get dirty. In a nearby village, Mr Li was to officially launch the water scheme by digging part of an irrigation ditch himself. When we arrived, there were several hundred bureaucrats waiting patiently. All were standing in lines behind placards that indicated which government department they came from.

Mr Li gave another speech, although this one was mercifully much shorter. He then picked up his shovel and pushed it into the earth to dig out the first clod of soil. I kept wondering why all these people had turned up. It wasn't until a little later that I found out why, when Mr Li left me alone in his office and I glanced at some papers on his desk. One was a notice that had been sent to departmental heads, warning them that anyone who didn't show up for the village ceremony would be publicly named and shamed on local television. So, that's why there were so many people and that's why they looked so bored; they'd had no choice but to watch Mr Li digging a ditch.

Mr Li's afternoon schedule was equally revealing. He was due to preside over the election of four people who would act as his deputies. An election in China; I was genuinely excited. Non-Chinese friends often ask me whether Chinese people would like to experience democracy. It's a difficult question to answer because while people in China know they do not have multi-party elections, many are still under the impression that their country is democratic. The communist party tells its citizens that it practises a kind of democracy in which it listens to what people have to say before making a decision, which everyone then has to follow. The party argues that this is democratic because people are, in theory, allowed to voice their opinions and influence the final outcome. This might be a different democracy to the one practised in the West, but China's rulers maintain that it's still democracy. To reinforce their democratic credentials, the authorities hold all kinds of elections for low-level positions and conduct them with great seriousness. The party's point of view is superficially persuasive and contains a grain of truth. China's leaders do respond to what people are thinking, as they've shown by introducing stricter environmental policies following growing concern about air pollution. But if the point of an election is to choose someone for a particular position in a free and fair vote from a range of candidates, then a Chinese election falls some way short of the ideal, as I was to find out.

The first problem with the election in Ningxia was that there were only four candidates for four positions, so no choice. The second problem was that the hopefuls were introduced as the new deputies even before the vote had taken place. That announcement came at a communist party meeting held slightly before the vote. It was organised for a visiting dignitary, who showed his disdain for the audience by keeping them all waiting. As proceedings were about to start, the VIP guest received a call on his mobile phone. I watched from the back of the room as, instead of declining to take it, he started chatting away. In China, top officials can do whatever they want without fear of criticism from those below. So as not to inconvenience everyone else gathered in the room, or more plausibly to keep his conversation to himself, he stood up and walked behind a curtain at the back of the room. Everyone else sat very still and waited, listening to every word that came from the booming voice of the visitor. He eventually finished the call and came back into the main room, retaking his seat on the stage, a signal for proceedings to continue. No one seemed perturbed by the disruption – but then a little later no one seemed concerned that the candidates were brought onto the stage and introduced as Mr Li's deputies even before the election.

With the decision already announced, all that remained was for the vote to take place. Mr Li shuffled his deputies into another room, where several dozen delegates were waiting to cast their ballots. When these were counted the candidates were confirmed in the positions that they'd already been told they would get. As we left the room, I wanted to ask Mr Li whether he thought that by announcing the names of his new deputies *before* the election he'd put the cart before the horse. I thought the metaphor might not translate well into Chinese, so instead I decided to ask him if any candidate in the county had ever been rejected. 'Never,' he beamed with obvious pride. He seemed pleased that the process had been successfully completed without a hitch. It didn't seem to concern Mr Li – perhaps it didn't occur to him – that the election had been a pointless procedure in the first place.

None of these inconsistencies were Mr Li's fault. As a person he seemed genuinely to care about the 200,000 or so people in his charge. In the hours before his long speech that morning, he'd tried to solve the various problems of numerous callers to his office, including a headteacher who had borrowed money to pay staff salaries and could not now pay it back. Towards the end of the day, Mr Li had also shown me the put-up bed that he'd set up for himself in a room next to his office. Sometimes he worked so late that there was no point going home. Mr Li was also proud of being a member of the communist party. On a wall in his office was a framed photograph of him and other Ningxia party members lined up with a previous president of China, Hu Jintao. The contradictions within Chinese politics were not Mr Li's making. He was simply a junior official trying to navigate a complex system. After just one day, I could see that China is bureaucratic; that decisions are often taken elsewhere by people more important; and that there are a lot of meaningless events to attend.

If Mr Li was just a small cog in a well-oiled machine, he was not the only one. Each March, the Chinese government holds its annual parliamentary session and thousands of delegates arrive in Beijing from across the country for the week-long jamboree. They approve government decisions taken during the previous year and look over its plans for the coming one. For a foreign reporter, it's a tired and tiring event. The schedule, the speeches and the decisions are all so predictable that, looking back, it's difficult to distinguish one year's meeting from another. Although some debate appears to go on behind the scenes, delegates have never voted down any proposal or work report put forward by the government, so many overseas journalists have fallen into the understandable habit of referring to the gathering as a rubber-stamp parliament. It's a term that annoys the Chinese government, which maintains the position that the parliament is an integral part of the country's democratic system. It's a stand-off between those who claim the gathering is a real event and those who think it's a sham. But who's right? I always wanted to answer that question in a way that would get as near to the truth as possible, and I thought I might have a chance with a new delegate called Hu Xiaoyan.

Hu Xiaoyan was briefly well known in China when she became the first-ever migrant worker to be selected as a delegate to the national parliament. Migrant workers are farmers who, over the last few decades, have left their homes in their hundreds of millions for better paid jobs in China's booming cities. Mrs Hu had originally come from Sichuan province in western China, but when I met her she was working in a factory that made ceramic tiles in the city of Foshan in southern Guangdong, one of China's richest provinces. The communist party had made a big deal of Mrs Hu's elevation to the national parliament, claiming it showed how all sectors of Chinese society were involved in the decision-making process. But how much power did she really have? On a trip to Guangdong for another story I decided to find her and ask her that question. I thought I might be able to find out more from Mrs Hu because she was relatively new to government, and I was hoping she would have the open and honest attitude often displayed by China's poorest people. Most officials, particularly the more senior ones, are usually very secretive about the process of governing. I thought Mrs Hu might not be.

She wasn't an easy woman to find. She was busy, and my colleague and I sat outside her tile factory all day waiting for her to come back from an appointment, but when we did finally meet her she was as welcoming as I'd initially imagined. She led us through the factory to a dormitory where she and her husband shared two small rooms. It was part home, part office. Papers were piled up on the bed and a small table with a laptop on it had been pushed against a wall. Her life, like those of all migrant workers, was filled with the kind of hardship that Westerners would struggle to accept. Mrs Hu had two daughters back home in Sichuan and when I saw her she hadn't seen them for two years. I immediately conjured up the faces of my two young children back in Beijing – my wife and I had added a daughter since arriving in China – and wondered what it might feel like not to see them for a full 24 months.

The previous year had not been an easy one for Mrs Hu. There had been a dispute at the factory between workers and management over money, and the new national delegate had been caught in the middle. The workers had expected her to push their claims, but she admitted that in the eyes of the factory's boss she was just like everyone else: a migrant worker. And then came an admission that Mrs Hu was still too innocent to know not to reveal to a journalist. She said that as a national parliamentary delegate she had no real power; she was simply told what to do. Her job was to pass on complaints to higher officials and ensure decisions made at the top were passed back down the chain of command. It didn't strike Mrs Hu as odd because that's the way things have always been done in China under the communists. She had been chosen as a national delegate by those in charge, not elected by the people, and so to her it seemed completely natural that she would have to do as she was told.

Meeting the county leader and the national parliamentary delegate left me feeling that I still hadn't got to the bottom of how China is governed. Both of these diligent officials worked hard, but they laboured without any real power. I needed to speak to someone higher up the food chain, but that's not easy to do in China because national leaders have largely closed themselves off from the outside world. They don't give interviews as Western political leaders do, and they say little about how they arrive at their decisions. Basic facts such as where they live and how much they get paid are treated as national secrets. A former general secretary of the communist party, Zhao Ziyang, had once annoyed his colleagues by giving an insight into the process of governing China. In 1989 he told the visiting leader of the Soviet Union, Mikhail Gorbachev, that Deng Xiaoping was the man in charge, even though at the time Deng was supposed to have retired from frontline politics. Many observers had guessed this to be the case all along, but until then no one senior had spoken so publicly about the issue. The revelation stands out because it's rare to find similar examples of plain speaking from a Chinese leader. One Western diplomat I spoke to likened China's political system to a big black hole; people peer inside, but see very little.

The only person close to the top of the ladder that I'd had the chance to observe was Madam Fu Ying. English-speaking, well-dressed and elegant, Madam Fu had been the Chinese ambassador in London before returning to China to become a vice-minister in the foreign affairs department. She talks fluently and convincingly about China's rise and its place in the world. Her soft voice, unthreatening manner and good looks help to show China in its best light. She's also a skilled diplomat, refusing to be drawn into conversations that might reveal too much or give the wrong kind of impression. Chinese leaders are not known for their light touch and sometimes struggle to find the right words to speak to their own people, never mind foreigners. Not Madam Fu. One of the few women in what is mostly a man's world, she manages to make China sound reasonable and benign. It might be, but she certainly makes it seem so. Interestingly, she's one of the few Chinese politicians – men or women – who appear happy to let their hair go grey. Most leaders, however elderly, maintain a thick, jet-black head of hair that's regularly coloured, presumably to suggest youth and vitality. Usually, only retired politicians, or those who've been arrested and so denied the necessary dye, appear in public without a coloured mane.

When she was still the ambassador in London, Madam Fu made a gift to the British Museum that sums up all her qualities as a diplomat. She presented the museum with food coupons that had been used by Chinese people to acquire basic provisions – rice, noodles and cloth – well into the

1980s. They were essentially ration cards, issued at a time when the Chinese government was not yet confident it could feed its people. The coupons handed over by Madam Fu had been kept by her mother, who had neatly tied them up with string and wrapped them in a handkerchief. She'd kept them long after they'd been phased out, just in case the bad times returned and they would once more prove useful. Before she died, Madam Fu's mother handed them to her daughter. 'She said I might need them again.' These simple pieces of paper neatly convey the idea that China's economy has travelled a great distance, from shortages to relative wealth, in just a few decades. They remind the world that poverty in China was recent. There are probably many people who can remember the rumble of an empty stomach. For a few, they still have to endure that uncomfortable feeling. Madam Fu seemed to be suggesting that her country ought to be given a little leeway as it catches up with the West.

She gave a similar message to Britain's Baroness Ashton when she visited China in her role as the European Union's foreign policy chief. She took the guest not to one of China's glittering cities, but to rural Guizhou, one of the poorest places in the country. The message was clear: just because China as a whole is rich, it doesn't mean there are not size-able pockets of deprivation. To ram home the point, the British visitor was shown the inside of tiny village homes and watched a group of scruffy children in a sparsely furnished classroom. 'Do you think you understand China without seeing this?' asked Madam Fu rhetorically, as she waved her arms to indicate the beautiful but poor mountain village we were ambling through. Madam Fu was trying to impress upon the European official that her country still had much to do and needed to be given time to do it. A good point well made, and one that Baroness Ashton later told me she'd understood.

That was the outward face of Madam Fu. In less public engagements she sometimes gave glimpses of the steel that must run through all senior communist party officials, who have somehow managed to climb to the top of a nation of more than one billion people. One British diplomat admitted that foreign officials who do business with Madam Fu were attracted by her charm and grace, but at the same time slightly afraid of her intellect and occasional caustic comment. I saw a flash of that anger at a briefing she gave to foreign journalists in Beijing, ahead of a planned meeting between Chinese and European officials. At the time, Europe's single currency, the *euro*, was going through a difficult period and more than one analyst suggested Beijing might be able to help.

China, with its strong economy and financial prudence, seemed for the moment to occupy the moral high ground and Madam Fu was quick to exploit it. She lectured the journalists, telling them that China had shown financial responsibility and Europeans should follow suit. Warming to her task, she went on to claim that her own nation would never repeat the mistakes of other world powers, who'd tried to impose their opinions and systems on weaker countries. She said China was different and, by implication, better. To me, these unguarded comments offered a different and less pleasant view of the vice-minister.

But even Madam Fu is, ultimately, just a functionary.

The foreign minister himself, her boss, is not even in the communist party's politburo, the decision-making body at the top of the party's organisational chart that graced the walls of the BBC's Beijing office. The men who rule China remain distant, two-dimensional figures seen on television greeting foreign dignitaries at airports or on conference podiums performing robotic speeches. It's not that their world cannot be understood; they must understand it very well. It's simply that they keep it hidden from everyone but the small group of people in their inner circle. They can maintain this secrecy because they don't have to undergo the inconvenience of real elections. If they needed people's votes they would have to be more open but, as they don't, they can carry on as they've always done, making sure politics is a game played by only a small elite. They appear to feel that they will face no serious challenge to their rule as long as the economy is doing well and as long as most people's lives are getting better. They are probably right in that assessment.

Later, I realised I'd been wrong to think that Madam Fu was the only senior leader I'd met during my time in China. I'd forgotten about Bao Tong because by the time I interviewed him he'd been stripped of power and was being watched 24 hours a day by the security services. He was a virtual prisoner in his own apartment, followed every time he left home, even for a trip to the supermarket. It hadn't always been like that. In the 1980s Bao Tong had been an adviser to Zhao Ziyang, the Chinese leader who'd told Mikhail Gorbachev that Deng Xiaoping was really the man in charge. In the late 80s Mr Zhao had risen to become the general secretary of the Chinese Communist Party. On paper at least this is the top job. Looking back, that time stands out as the most open decade of the communist party's rule. It was just after the Cultural Revolution and there was genuine public debate about how China should change. All things seemed possible. Zhao Ziyang was driving that movement from his position at the top of the party and Bao Tong was one of his trusted advisers. He'd been far closer to the centre of power than Madam Fu.

Of course, we now know how that optimism played out: with the massacre that ended the protests in Tiananmen Square in 1989. A few weeks before the killing, Zhao Ziyang was arrested and disappeared from public view; his colleagues thought he'd been too sympathetic towards the students and their demands. He remained in detention until his death in 2005. There's a grainy black and white photograph of Mr Zhao taken in Tiananmen Square just a few days before his fall from power. He'd gone there to plead with the students. In the picture the leader looks forlorn and tired, as though he already knows the game is up. When Mr Zhao went, those around him inevitably came under suspicion, including Bao Tong. The demise of this one adviser reveals the speed and ruthlessness with which the party can act when it's fighting for its own survival.

It happened on 28th May. A Sunday. Bao Tong was eating lunch when the telephone rang. He was being summoned to a politburo meeting. Zhao Ziyang had disappeared a few days before, leaving Mr Bao with nothing to do, no documents to read and no one to give advice to. He suspected there really was no politburo meeting, but he had no choice but to go. 'I'll wait for my driver to come back,' he told the person on the other end of the line. 'No, no. Don't wait. We'll send a car.' When he arrived at where he'd been told to go, Bao Tong was met by a man called Song Ping, one of the ageing revolutionaries who were still making all the important political decisions, even though many of them were supposed to have retired.

Song Ping asked about Bao Tong's security and wondered whether he might be attacked by the students. He seemed concerned and asked Mr Bao to move into Zhongnanhai, a palace complex in the heart of Beijing that was built by China's emperors and is now used by the country's top communist leaders. Finally, Mr Song took his colleague's hand and shook it long and hard. He said goodbye. Waiting outside the meeting room was a car that Bao Tong didn't recognise, it certainly wasn't his own. It had *GA* written on the side. *GA* for *Gong An*, China's public security bureau, its police force. The Tiananmen protests were still going on and

Mr Bao was driven through streets crowded with people. Occasionally, there was no way through and they would have to double back. It was difficult to work out where they were going and no one bothered to tell Mr Bao. 'Then we came to a compound and I said, "Is this Qincheng?" Someone said, "Yes".'

Qincheng is a jail on the outskirts of Beijing reserved for political prisoners. It was to be Bao Tong's home for the next seven years. The adviser's speedy fall from power is a cautionary tale for anyone taken in by the Chinese Communist Party's more reasonable face, as presented by skilled diplomats such as Madam Fu. Bao Tong's experiences remind us that the party is at heart a ruthless machine whose main objective is to survive.

The complexities of China's political system, and the machinations at the top of the communist party, were not something that concerned the teacher while he was still working in the MSG factory. He was more interested in how to escape to a better life. Fortunately for him, China's leaders had also been thinking about how to provide an education for people just like him. They knew only too well that during the Cultural Revolution millions of youngsters had simply stopped going to school and were now wasting their potential in unsuitable jobs. In 1977, the year after Mao died, schools and universities returned to normal and gradually those who'd missed out returned to their books. The teacher was one of them. He came to realise that his long-held dream of going to university could become a reality. But the right to study was not guaranteed and the teacher had to fight to change his life.

The first hurdle was to pass the university entrance exam, held just once a year. The teacher managed to persuade his factory to give him time off to revise. He also attended evening classes in a desperate attempt to plug the gaps in his knowledge. Finally, in 1984, when he was already in his early thirties, the teacher took the test. He passed, but then another obstacle suddenly appeared. More than a dozen workers had successfully sat the exam at the same time, but the factory would only allow a handful of them to go to university. Who would be chosen? In the end, it was the ones with the best connections, mostly those who'd been bosses themselves, who were allowed to go. The teacher and the other workers who'd passed the exam were furious and complained to a higher authority. Understandably, the factory managers were not too pleased to hear their judgement was being questioned and punished the troublemakers by sending them to work in the countryside for a couple of months, planting trees. But the complaining worked; that autumn the teacher was allowed to go to university.

If anyone ever cares to search out the world's most august institutions of learning, they will probably not come across the Beijing No 2 Commercial Employees' University. It was set up specifically for mature students who'd missed out on university because of the Cultural Revolution. The teacher studied factory management. His employers paid his fees and gave him a small monthly allowance on the understanding that he would go back and work at the factory at the end of the three-year course. The teacher was overjoyed. He had freedom, a little money and the chance to study. Life was beginning to look up.

Visiting Mao

I met the teacher at Beijing's western railway station under a glorious evening sun. He was wearing the outfit he usually wore when dressed as a man: loose-fitting trousers held up by a belt, topped off with a white shirt. It's the kind of informal uniform seen on many men of his age, from the lowest office worker to leaders of the country. The teacher was pulling a small suitcase with a pink ribbon attached to the handle. At the time, he hadn't yet told me about his cross-dressing, but if I'd been looking for hints about who he really was I should perhaps have thought more about the ribbon.

We were off to see Chairman Mao or, to be more accurate, to visit the former leader's hometown. So much of the teacher's story involves the Great Helmsman that we decided to find out what we could about where Mao came from; to find out what propelled the son of a farmer to rule the world's most populous country. The teacher's attitude towards the Chairman intrigued me. His views about Mao were no different to those of many other people in China, but it didn't stop me wondering why he held them. Chairman Mao had initiated a series of policies that had ended, ruined or severely disrupted the lives of tens of millions – but most people still admired him, or at least respected what he'd achieved in the early part of his career. After Mao's death and the end of the Cultural Revolution, the communist party had come to its own amazingly precise verdict on the former leader. It declared that he'd been 70 per cent right and 30 per cent wrong. It was a conclusion that most people accepted as the truth. The teacher knew perfectly well that his early life had been turned upside down by Mao, but he still admired him anyway. How could that be?

We travelled south to the city of Changsha in Hunan province, near to Mao's hometown of Shaoshan. It would have been quicker to fly, but taking the train in China is far more fun and we were in no rush, so we again found ourselves in one of China's cavernous railway stations, observing the usual collection of humanity waiting patiently to board their trains. A couple cuddled as they stood among a crowd of hundreds. They seemed oblivious to everyone else around them. The young woman was gently picking at her partner's face, pulling off what seemed like pieces of dead skin. He had bad acne so there was plenty of material to work with. On a bench was a group of craggy-faced migrant workers wearing the dirty, ill-fitting clothes that adorn poor people the world over. They had no luggage to speak of; their belongings were simply crammed into sacks that were tied up with string. In another part of the waiting room a man without arms was begging for change.

I was preparing to leave China and this was going to be one of my last train journeys, so when we got on board I spent some time looking round, trying to etch into my memory all the usual, everyday sights that had seemed so odd when I'd first arrived in the country. These things would no doubt seem like distant memories as soon as I left. Travellers have been fascinated by different cultures ever since they first took to the road, but we seem to have little collective memory and each generation experiences the thrill of travel anew. As I looked round the crowded carriage, it struck me that there are many ways to live a life, and the difference between normal and strange can sometimes come down to a simple matter of perspective. It wasn't a unique insight; many others have observed the same thing before me, but I was still pleased that China had given me the opportunity to see something different.

As the teacher and I settled down in our first-class compartment, the talk inevitably turned to Mao. 'If you take the long view of history, he was a great man,' said a well-dressed gentleman who was sharing our travelling space. The man had originally come from Hunan, but was now living in Beijing. He owned a restaurant that sold dishes from his native region. With great pride, he told us that its speciality was roast suckling pig. He handed over a name card and told us to drop by when we returned to the capital. I couldn't help thinking that the kind of free enterprise the man was engaged in would not have been viewed favourably by the Chairman, but the restaurateur was beginning to warm to the conversation and I didn't want to stop his flow.

He said Mao's greatest achievement had been to secure the land. He could be right. It's hard to imagine now, but in the early part of the twentieth century China was in danger of breaking apart. Different regions were ruled by different warlords. There was a nationalist government and communist insurgents and the Japanese were slowly nibbling away at territory in the northeast. When he took power, Mao unified the country for the first time in decades. By putting it back together, the argument goes, he laid the foundations for what came later: Deng Xiaoping, the elderly leader who cleaned up after the Cultural Revolution and opened China to the outside world. The well-dressed man who now owned a restaurant was pleased with his country's growing strength and said so. But then he suddenly looked at me and seemed to check his pride. He leaned over and in a more serious tone said China would never be like Britain and the United States; it would never have colonies or attack other countries. 'It's just not part of our culture,' he said with a certainty that I didn't share. I wondered how many people from other rising powers had said something similar.

During a lull in our conversation I realised that Madam Fu, the former Chinese ambassador to Britain, had talked in exactly the same vein. She'd also said that China would never seek to impose itself on others. Madam Fu would have been impressed with the man in the train compartment. His views and those of the government that ruled over him were in perfect harmony. In truth, it wasn't an unusual situation to come across. On the big political issues in China there's almost complete uniformity of thinking. Should Taiwan, a self-governing island off the eastern seaboard, really be incorporated into China? Of course it should. It's been Chinese since ancient times. Should Tibet be allowed to become an independent country? Of course not. It's been ruled by China since ancient times. Is the South China Sea an inherent part of Chinese territory? Of course it is. Chinese fishermen have been plying the waters there since ancient times. The answers to these and many more questions were always the same. Eventually I gave up asking them; there was simply nothing new to learn.

From the outside looking in, it isn't hard to work out why almost everyone has the same point of view. The communist party has a virtual monopoly on information, which it begins feeding to its citizens in nursery school. The party runs or controls everything that might offer a different perspective; television, newspapers, magazines, books, films, the internet, even art galleries. No platform is given to opposition politicians; there aren't any. There are no independent trade unions, and civil rights groups that could encourage public debate do not exist. Those that do somehow manage to form are usually hounded into submission. There might have once been some wiggle room for an alternative opinion from organisations that focused on specific issues, such as the environment, but under the current President, Xi Jinping, even that space has been closed up. So is it strange that most people think the same way? Not really.

Occasionally, I'd try a different tactic in order to get someone to realise that there's more than one valid viewpoint. I'd sometimes ask Chinese people what discussions were like in their own families when they were talking about non-political issues, say, the best place to go for dinner. 'Oh, we always argue,' would be a common reply. 'My dad says one thing, but my mother rarely agrees. My grandparents always say something else entirely.' I would then interject with what I naively thought was a killer line: if there are so many points of view in just one family about an issue as simple as where to eat, don't you think it's odd that more than a billion people all share the same opinion about whether Taiwan is a part of China? The first few times I tried this approach I'd be convinced that I really had revealed other possibilities. I was sadly mistaken. Whoever I was questioning would usually pause for a few moments before saying, with the complete confidence of someone who's right: 'Yes, but Taiwan is a part of China. It has been since ancient times.'

By the time the teacher and I were travelling to Hunan I'd learned to keep my own counsel, so I didn't challenge the restaurateur about his views on Chairman Mao. But I wasn't always so relaxed about China's cultural differences, and I was reminded of that as our train chugged slowly towards Changsha sometime before dawn. I was woken up by an attendant as she came through the carriage noisily emptying the rubbish bins in each compartment. She wasn't even pretending to work quietly. During nearly seven decades of rule, the communists have promoted the idea that the collective nature of society is far more important than the individuals in it. So it was probably normal for the attendant to think only of the general good of cleaning the carriage and not worry too much about whether she was disturbing the sleep of anyone in particular. My fellow train travellers, perhaps more conditioned to this kind of behaviour, didn't seem to mind. They were being stoical in the face of something they could do nothing about. They'd probably calculated that it was better to simply ignore the annoying aspects of life, such as a noisy train cleaner, rather than try and fail to do something about it.

Other small things happened on the train that also struck me as plain wrong. As I lifted myself up from my bed, I saw a sign urging passengers to be careful when choosing a place to spit inside the sealed carriage. Spitting in public has only in recent years started to become a taboo in Chinese society and many people still cling to this traditional habit, so it would have been pointless to ask passengers not to spit at all. The best the authorities could do was to get them to think about where to do it. I was wondering, with a slight shudder of disgust, just where that place might be when from somewhere deep inside the carriage I heard the familiar sound of someone fetching something up from the bottom of their throat. It was a sound of China, but not one I liked. A few minutes later, as I was brushing my teeth in a small basin at the end of the carriage, I noticed a 'no smoking' sign tacked to the wall. Despite the warning, a large man next to me was skilfully cleaning his teeth and smoking a cigarette at the same time. As I admired his dexterity, he leaned across and tapped his ash into my sink. He said nothing by way of explanation. He just collected his things and slowly walked away. I was left fuming. But afterwards I wondered whether the spitting and the ash flicking really were so wrong. Was it just my different upbringing that had brought me to that conclusion?

The teacher was by this time already up and dressed. I

hadn't spotted the significance of the pink ribbon the night before and, in a similar act of oversight, I failed to think properly about the necklace that was hanging around his neck and displayed outside his clothing. It was a piece of jade in the shape of a teardrop, held in a delicate silver clasp.

After jumping down from the train, we headed off to find a tour group that would take us to Mao's hometown. Guides gather round the station waiting for customers from the overnight trains and it wasn't difficult to find one. In another ironic twist in communist China, there was intense competition among the various firms that take tourists to see Chairman Mao's former home. Competition to see a communist was not something Mao himself would have imagined. We signed up with the first guide who approached us and were taken to join a small gaggle of other visitors who were already waiting for a tour bus to arrive.

As we waited I observed my fellow travellers, including a middle-aged couple from the city of Wuhan who were busy complaining about the ugly architecture in Changsha. Before long, they fell into conversation with the teacher. I've always admired the way complete strangers in China can start talking to each other as though they are long-lost friends, and the teacher's easy manner with these new acquaintances reminded me of this endearing trait. He told the couple that his son had once had a girlfriend from Wuhan and then, without a hint of embarrassment, added: 'I wanted them to split up because I didn't want him to marry someone from outside Beijing.' I squirmed, but the couple didn't bat an eyelid. Perhaps the teacher had judged the situation correctly, knowing his comments would not be taken as an insult. Still, the couple didn't bother speaking to us for the rest of the trip.

Once on board, we had barely passed the outer limits of Changsha when our tour guide piped up for the first time.

With a microphone attached to her head and a speaker fastened to her hip, Young Li had a few housekeeping items she wanted to get cleared up. Firstly, the road. It was currently being re-laid and was not in the best condition. 'Keep safe, particularly those at the back,' she shouted. 'It could get bumpy.' Perhaps her comments would have been better addressed at the driver, who seemed not to hear as he pressed on as if his life depended on arriving early. Secondly, Young Li wanted to talk about the journey home, which would take one and a half hours if we took the usual route or just an hour if we used the new motorway. The guide explained that our ticket price did not include the fee for the toll on the faster motorway. 'That's how we keep it so cheap,' she explained. We would have to pay an extra 35 yuan (£3.50) between us if we wanted to get back to Changsha half an hour earlier than scheduled. Could everyone club together? Young Li asked how many were in favour of paying a little more. Immediately a forest of hands shot into the air. In all my time in China it was the only occasion I ever saw a free and fair vote.

All tours in China take place at speed and there's never much time to contemplate this or that. This trip was no different. It wasn't long before we arrived at our first stop, a ceremonial hall that contained a golden statue of the tour's hero, Mao Zedong. Before we were allowed off, Young Li told us we had to remember three numbers. The first was 05988, the licence plate of the bus we were travelling on. As I've already mentioned, Young Li's company wasn't the only one ferrying tourists to see Mao that day; the car park was crammed full of coaches that all looked very similar. 'Remember that number so you'll know where to come back to,' she barked. The second group of digits to remember was her mobile telephone number, just in case we got lost. And finally, we had to commit to memory 11.40am because that was the time we were due back on the bus. 'Don't be late or we'll leave without you,' she said helpfully.

Inside the hall our small group of tourists began to resemble a respectful huddle of pilgrims. Mao's statue was housed in a small room and we carefully stepped towards it in neat lines of nine. I felt uncomfortable honouring a man who'd killed so many, so I moved to one side and watched as the others bowed three times to show their respect. They were each handed a small golden coin while bending their bodies at the waist. I wondered about the coin's significance as we were ushered into an adjoining room to make way for the next group. The matter was immediately cleared up. In this anteroom assistants sat behind a long desk and for a small fee they would engrave each coin with the owner's name and the date of the visit. It was not the first time, not even the first time that day, that I'd noticed how piety and commerce so often exist side by side in China.

Piety was a word that kept cropping up throughout the day. Mao had not been an imaginary figure, but a real man who'd done real things, a lot of them bad. But for many Chinese people he's become a god-like figure, imbued with mythical powers. The story of Mao's statue, which stands in a small park near his childhood home, is a perfect example. It was erected in 1993 to commemorate the centenary of the Chairman's birth and is a focal point for tourists. Young Li allowed us only a minute or two to walk through the park because we were behind schedule, but throughout the day she kept telling us remarkable stories about the giant bronze statue. It had arrived on the back of a lorry that had made a slow journey to Shaoshan, stopping along the way at various sites associated with Mao. When it got to Jinggangshan, the revolutionary base area set up by Mao and his comrade Zhu De in 1927, the engine on the brand new lorry had suddenly shuddered to a halt. Nothing could induce it to start again.

The dignitaries leading the trip decided it was Mao's doing – despite the fact that he'd been dead for 17 years. They thought the great man wanted to spend one last night in the area, so they stayed. According to legend, in the morning the driver got back into the lorry and turned the key. The engine fired up the first time without any problem. Satisfied and refreshed, Mao had apparently allowed the procession to continue.

The miracles didn't stop there. Young Li said the statue had arrived in Shaoshan in winter, to be greeted by thousands of cheering people and flowers that had suddenly opened, despite the cold. The sun and the moon appeared in the sky together. And if anyone was in any doubt that Mao was orchestrating events from beyond the grave, there was one final piece of evidence. Jiang Zemin, the man who was then president of China, presided over the official unveiling of the statue. Young Li said that when Mr Jiang stepped forward to reveal the work of art to the assembled gathering, the red covering would not come off. So he stepped back and bowed three times and then tried again. It doesn't take a genius to guess the ending of the story – the veil instantly slipped off. Did anyone believe these stories? It didn't really matter. Even when he was still alive, Mao Zedong was more than living flesh and blood, and that hadn't changed in the years since his death.

That's not to say that while he was still breathing Mao was above the day-to-day issues that trouble lesser mortals. He no doubt felt a draught from an open door like the rest of us, and enjoyed the material delights that fame, fortune and untrammelled power can bring. That much is clear from the two houses that dominate Shaoshan: Mao's childhood home and the villa that was built for him nearby in later life. The two homes chart the course of a man who began his life as a peasant and ended it as the leader of China.

The family home where Mao grew up is a spacious one-storey building made of light-coloured bricks and black tiles. Some parts of the roof are thatched. Behind there's a low, wooded hill and in front there's a pond, where Mao would go swimming as a boy. As the sun shone down on our small tour group as we waited to enter, I couldn't help thinking that the house looked like a city dweller's dream of ideal country living. It's clear from the house that the Mao family had not been the poorest farmers in the district. Mao admitted as much on a trip back to his old home in 1959. He told his personal doctor that had his father been alive then, he would have been classified as a rich peasant and 'struggled against', which was just another way of saying persecuted.

Of course, life hadn't been entirely easy for the Mao family, as it wasn't for most of the other people who lived in rural China at the end of the nineteenth century. Just getting by must have been tough. It was difficult to get a feel for this poverty though because Mao's childhood home has probably changed a great deal over the years. A sign near the entrance made it clear that it had gone through a series of renovations since the communist party took power in 1949. What we were looking at seemed to say little about the struggles of Mao's young life, beyond the fact that he grew up in the countryside and it was not the most prosperous of beginnings.

It's easier to see Mao's personality from the second home he's associated with in Shaoshan. *Dishuidong*, or *Dripping Water Cave*, is a sprawling villa built at the end of a beautiful gorge and surrounded by a bamboo forest. It's a rural retreat fit for an emperor, just a few miles from Mao's childhood home. Mao had once said he intended to retire to Shaoshan and live in a thatched cottage. In response, local leaders had built *Dripping Water Cave*. They obviously had an instinctive feel for what China's leader might mean by 'thatched cottage', and wisely did not take his words literally. Mao might have grown up in relative poverty in the 1890s, but by the time his Shaoshan villa was built in the 1960s he had fully embraced the joys of modern living.

Before the communists took over, troops from Mao's red army had mostly been uneducated farmers and when they'd arrived in Shanghai, a cosmopolitan city that had been under foreign control, they'd encountered some unusual items. One story, perhaps apocryphal, retells the moment soldiers discovered a bidet in the bathroom of one of Shanghai's luxury hotels. Not knowing what it was for, they washed their rice rations in it. Things had changed by the time Mao's Shaoshan villa was built. Communist leaders had once lived in caves dug out of hillsides, but the benefits of a flush toilet later managed to penetrate the upper echelons of the party. Workers had installed advanced plumbing in Mao's bathroom in the villa. The toilet, sink and bath had been imported from the Soviet Union, then Beijing's ally, because nothing of a similar standard could be found in China.

A notice hung up outside Mao's bedroom gives another indication of the kind of person he had by then become. It said Mao's main activities when he'd stayed at the villa had been resting and reading, and so his underlings had designed and built a special wooden bed that allowed him to do both at the same time. It was raised up at one side so the leader of China could put his books there when he'd done with them, knowing they would be handily by his side when he'd finished sleeping and wanted them again. As I looked at the bed I was reminded of another sign, at Mao's childhood home, which told visitors that when he was a young man the future leader of China had developed a deep love of physical labour. The bed at *Dripping Water Cave* made me think that Mao's love of manual work, even if it had existed, had certainly not stayed with him. By the time he ruled China he couldn't be bothered to get up and put his books away.

Another thing struck me about *Dripping Water Cave*. It was built between 1960 and 1962, a time when China was still in what was perhaps its most tragic famine. No one is exactly sure how many people starved to death because the communist party keeps a lid on the figures and doesn't want the issue discussed, but most credible estimates believe tens of millions of people died. The party still maintains the lie that it was caused by a natural disaster, but the truth is far more horrible: it was man-made. Mao, desperate to push China into a higher stage of communism, had forced rural people into communes in 1958, in a campaign known as the *Great Leap Forward*. The disruption – chaos would perhaps be a better word – led to a disastrous fall in crop yields and widespread famine. But while millions of people were starving, a luxurious villa was being built for Mao in his hometown. That's not all. Work continued over the next couple of years on improvements, a time when the rest of China was still struggling to overcome the effects of the famine. The villa was given rooms that could protect Mao against bombs, radiation and earthquakes; everyone else was worrying about the more mundane problem of where to find something to eat.

How could Mao have allowed so many local resources to be diverted into something he didn't really need? It wasn't as though he didn't know of the difficulties faced by people living in the district where he'd grown up. His visit to Shaoshan in 1959 had been made partly to see how his new political campaign was panning out. Was it a great leap forward? What he heard from local people, unafraid to speak to a man who'd once been one of their own, was truly shocking. Mao invited 50 of them to a banquet and they spent the whole evening complaining. As part of the political changes, communes across China had been instructed to build backyard furnaces in an attempt to increase steel production, and Shaoshan was no different. But the district had no iron ore and so local leaders had confiscated people's pots and pans and shovels and melted them down. This job required quite a lot of fuel, which was also in short supply. To solve the problem, party bosses ordered doors to be ripped from their frames and furniture seized from living rooms. It was all chopped up and thrown into the furnaces. Despite these enormous sacrifices, all those useful things were ultimately wasted. The backyard furnaces produced poor-quality steel ingots that no one knew what to do with. It must have taken Shaoshan years to recover. Mao had known all this and had still allowed local leaders to build him a villa.

Young Li, our guide, then casually dropped into conversation a telling fact, which seemed to render the building of the villa entirely pointless. She told us that Mao had actually spent just 12 days there, in 1966. Twelve days from 17th June to 28th June and of course, as our tour group already knew, Mao had spent much of that time reclining with books and papers on his specially made bed. Far from being embarrassed about the lack of time Mao spent at the villa, the management seemed proud of the fact. They'd written it all up and put it on a big red sign. I felt sorry for the people who had died of hunger while this luxurious villa was being built. But I consoled myself a little with the thought that the building was belatedly providing a return on its original investment, from the hundreds of tourists who pay each day to enter.

Later, as we continued wandering around the villa, I realised *Dripping Water Cave* had perhaps played a more important role in history than I'd first thought. I looked at the date of Mao's stay again: June 1966, a month after he'd launched the Cultural Revolution and just a few weeks before one of the most pivotal moments of his life. In the middle of July the seventy-two-year-old Mao joined 5,000 people in Wuhan for the annual swim across the Yangtze River. Over the previous few years, Mao had been sidelined by colleagues at the top of the party – mostly because of his disastrous *Great Leap Forward* – and he wasn't happy. He wanted to be in charge of shaping the country's destiny, and he was keen to show that he was still young and healthy enough to do it.

There's no better way to show your vitality then by taking a plunge in one of China's great rivers, so that's what he did. Mao didn't really swim the Yangtze, he just bobbed along, allowing the current to take him downstream for about ten miles as his anxious bodyguards floated along beside him. They were worried sick their boss might drown. Photographs that were later used as propaganda show the Chairman's head sticking out of the water, a relaxed almost smug expression on his face. Another picture shows Mao on the deck of a boat, wearing a bathrobe and waving to the crowd. Mao's dip in the river did its job. It re-established the Chairman's credentials and he returned to Beijing to wrest back control of the communist party. It was a personal triumph for Mao – but a terrible moment for China.

Mao practised his famous Yangtze swim in the reservoir at *Dripping Water Cave* in the stifling heat of that 12-day stay in June. A grainy film played on a constant loop in one of the villa's side rooms shows Mao being led into the water by three athletic-looking young men. The Chairman takes tentative steps as he wades further into the reservoir. He's wearing a pair of giant white trunks that are hoisted high to cover what had by then become a sizeable belly. Once in, Mao seemed at home, laughing for the camera that was recording his every move. Did he plan his rejuvenative swim in the Yangtze while at *Dripping Water Cave*?

I was fascinated, but the teacher was taking in the sights with the detached air of a man looking at things that had no personal connection to him. His young life had been ruined by Mao, but he showed little emotion as we traipsed around the former leader's villa. I asked him what he thought. 'I was as enthusiastic as anyone in the 1960s, but in the 80s I realised he was just a man like everyone else,' was all I could get out of him. The only time the teacher seemed to get angry was when we were leaving *Dripping Water Cave*. Young Li mentioned that the villa we'd just visited was only one of two built on the site. The second one had been completed, but never used. I asked her why we couldn't go into that one. 'It's not interesting,' she said. For some reason the existence of a second villa annoyed the teacher. 'What a waste of money,' he muttered. I couldn't help agreeing.

Contradictions can be found in all places, but I always felt they seem to exist more happily together in China. A person could do or say one thing one day and the opposite the next day, without any sense of hypocrisy. I remember how once, in one of the regular media briefings held by China's foreign ministry in Beijing, the spokesman had laughed when asked about an incident in which a shoe had been thrown at the then US President, George W Bush, at a news conference in Iraq. The Chinese spokesman's reply to the question had been something along the lines of: 'I better watch out when you lot bend down to tie your shoelaces; you might be getting something to throw at me.'

The spokesman thought a shoe hurled in anger at the US president was something to laugh about. Some time later a shoe was also thrown at Wen Jiabao, who was then China's premier, while he was on a tour of Britain and, again, journalists at the foreign ministry briefing asked a question about the incident. This time the attitude changed. The spokeswoman on duty that day was sombre and expressed the Chinese government's indignation at the insult shown towards its premier. I pointed out that the Chinese government had brushed aside a similar incident when it had happened to the US president. I then sat back and waited for her answer, confident that I had just shown how hypocritical the Chinese government could be when it came to the issue of throwing shoes at visiting dignitaries. But the spokeswoman quickly dismissed my comment. 'What was said then was correct and what I'm saying now is also correct,' she said and without pausing moved on to the next question.

The shoe-throwing anecdote is a rather long-winded way to say that it should have come as no surprise when, as part of our visit to the birthplace of Mao Zedong, we also stopped off at the childhood home of his greatest rival within the communist party, Liu Shaoqi, who just happened to have been brought up very close to where Mao was born. Though far less celebrated than Mao, Liu Shaoqi had shared the great leader's struggles throughout China's civil war and had once been the country's head of state. He was at one point second only to Mao in the communist party's pecking order. But the two men had different views about how China should develop and Liu Shaoqi was purged during the Cultural Revolution. He was beaten regularly by Mao's young Red Guards and denied proper medical treatment. He died in prison in 1969. He was posthumously rehabilitated and his family home is now a shrine to the former leader. It didn't seem to strike anyone as odd that two men once locked in a vicious battle for survival would one day become part of the same tourist trip, as though their differences had been a mere tiff now best forgotten. Young Li certainly didn't say why, on a tour to celebrate the life of Mao, we were visiting the home of a man who the Chairman had effectively killed. She left the issue unaddressed. 'Make sure you're not late for the bus,' was the comment she was most anxious to impress upon us.

China's current communist rulers have not forgotten what went on in the past and they admit there were some difficult times. After the Cultural Revolution ended those who most vigorously supported it were put in prison, including Mao's wife Jiang Qing. There was also a final assessment of that chaotic period. The communist party issued a verdict that ran something like this: OK, we did some bad things, but it's all over now and we've said we're sorry. Can we start again? The party knows that it doesn't serve any purpose to dwell on the past or to make too much fuss about what went on, even if it concerns the lives and deaths of millions of people. If they did that, China's citizens might start looking more closely at what the party is doing now. So, at Liu Shaoqi's home there's a celebration of his life, but little information about his demise. That odd situation is perfectly illustrated by the bronze statue of the great man that stands just outside his old home. The statue shows Liu Shaoqi striking a suitably revolutionary pose. One arm is placed defiantly on his hip as he gazes into the distance, presumably looking for a better future. Underneath there's a plaque, which mentions with obvious pride that the area in which the statue stands measures 8,000 square metres. It also points out that the statue itself is 7.1 metres high, a symbolic figure as 71 was the age at which Liu Shaoqi died. A series of unnecessary statistics, but no mention of how the former leader met his end, or why.

When I looked more closely though, I realised that the home does contain some evidence of the pain endured by Liu Shaoqi and his family in the Cultural Revolution. In a room of photographs there's a telling picture from 1967, when the Cultural Revolution was in full swing. In the picture Liu Shaoqi's wife, Wang Guangmei, is being humiliated in front of 30,000 students. A few years earlier, when she was effectively the first lady of China, this good-looking woman had attended a banquet in Indonesia wearing a *qipao*, a traditional Chinese dress with a high collar and slits up the sides.

The dress has a long history in China, but became particularly popular in Shanghai in the 1920s. It fell out of favour when the communists came to power partly because it seemed to represent the decadence of the time, a decadence they wanted to sweep out of China. The Red Guards did not forget that Wang Guangmei had once worn a *qipao* in Indonesia and used it against her in the struggle sessions she was forced to endure during the Cultural Revolution.

The photograph in her husband's former home shows her standing on a stage at Beijing's Qinghua University, with two Red Guards beside her. They are holding her arms and thrusting her forward. The former first lady had been forced to wear a *qipao* over her clothes and a necklace of ping pong balls had been placed around her neck, to mimic the pearls she'd also worn in Indonesia. The photograph shows a complex and humiliating scene, but why had the rally been held? What had happened to the people in it? How could the communist party ensure that something like this would never take place again? Sadly, there was little explanation below the photograph. It was just something that had happened and was now not happening.

In public, Mao's terrible actions during the Cultural Revolution are acknowledged, but glossed over. In less public places though I was surprised to learn there's more enthusiasm for the man whose policies led to so many deaths. I made that discovery about a year before our trip to Shaoshan when I visited the Chinese Academy of Governance in Beijing. It's a school for officials from across the country. They go there to hear about the party's latest thinking. When I visited, I saw dozens of bureaucrats sitting in an auditorium, like university students, listening to a professor deliver a lecture. It was entitled *The Art of Leadership and Political Wisdom of Mao Zedong*. The lecturer, and obviously his superiors who'd sanctioned the talk, believe China's former leader still has something to offer officials who govern today. After listening for a few minutes it was also clear that Mao is still thought of as a brilliant leader by many who currently run the country. The lecturer picked out Mao's ability to focus on big things and not get bogged down with trivial details, like a few million deaths I thought sarcastically. I suppose the experience of anyone who ruled that long – Mao was in charge of the Chinese Communist Party for four decades – might prove useful for future generations. But the open adulation for the former leader on show at the academy, in contrast to the more muted official comments in public, struck me as more than a little odd, and very telling.

The trip back to Changsha was, as the tour guide Young Li had predicted, quicker than the outward journey that morning. But I wouldn't have minded a longer bus ride because I was trying to work out what I thought about Mao. It's easier to come to conclusions about the two other great dictators of the twentieth century: Hitler and Stalin. Their crimes were so shocking that few people now defend them. But can we say the same for Mao? My own feelings on this subject are complex. Mao's policies certainly led to the deaths of tens of millions of people, but somehow he doesn't seem to be in the same league as those two other dictators.

I have a poster of Chairman Mao on the wall of my home; it's inconceivable that I'd put up a picture of Hitler or Stalin. The teacher had long ago accepted the communist party's own verdict on its former leader, that he was 70 per cent good and 30 per cent bad. His visit to Shaoshan had not changed that view one little bit. 'He was a great man, but he made mistakes,' was all he said on the way back to Changsha that evening. As I've already said, it was an opinion you heard all the time in China. The teacher was obviously aware that the course of his life had been changed for the worse by Mao, but any pain, regret or anger that he might once have felt was now gone. The teacher had believed in Mao, but now no longer did. For him, it was as simple as that.

Heng Mountain

It was in Changsha that evening, following our visit to Mao's hometown, that the teacher finally decided to let me see the other side of his personality. After the initial shock wore off, I lay in bed that night thinking about all the signs I'd overlooked. I realised that I'd seen enough over the years to at least raise questions in my mind. I felt rather annoyed with myself for failing to see what in retrospect seemed obvious. I was supposed to be a journalist, a trained observer, but I'd missed something big that had been right under my nose for some time. I was also a little disappointed the teacher had not confided in me earlier.

At least the ice had been broken and the teacher could now wear what he wanted, so when he came down to the hotel lobby the next morning he was clothed in what he'd had on the previous evening. I was still adjusting though, and stood awkwardly next to him as we took a bus to the long-distance coach station on the outskirts of Changsha. Few other people seemed to notice the teacher or, if they did, they didn't betray their feelings. Only a small girl, probably unused to seeing a man dressed as a woman in provincial China, asked why he was wearing make-up. Eventually, I put the issue to the back of my mind and got on with enjoying our journey. Our destination was Heng Mountain, one of China's five sacred peaks, just a few hours' drive from Changsha. The teacher wanted to go there so we could engage in one of the great

Chinese pastimes: walking up a big hill while admiring the scenery.

A simple bus ride anywhere in rural China reveals the energy that's been unleashed since the country began opening up to new ideas and the outside world in the 1980s. In the midst of all this change, the future and the past sit side by side, and through the bus window I could see where China was coming from and where it was going. As we drove towards Heng Mountain, remnants of an older, slower-paced China were still on show. There were wood-beamed houses like the one Chairman Mao had grown up in and farmers planting rice in flooded paddy fields. Chickens pecked at scraps around doorways, and along the side of the road people stood in small clusters chatting and smoking.

That China was being swept away, and there was another more modern country on view from the bus window. Coal trucks pushed through the traffic, delivering the energy that powers economic development. Outside roadside workshops were piles of bricks and mountains of scrap metal. Diggers sat idle beside a bulldozed pathway that would eventually become a new multi-lane thoroughfare and the skeletons of concrete buildings loomed over empty streets. To advertise the brand new apartments these buildings would eventually house were billboards showing comforting domestic scenes, which the developers no doubt hoped would tempt buyers. These adverts didn't just promise a new home, but also hinted at a new way of living, free from the poverty and deprivation of the past. It's a vision of the future that's been embraced completely in China. As our bus pulled up at a set of traffic lights, I noticed a car in front with a sign attached to the roof. 'Fixing leaks is our speciality,' it boasted in large red letters. Some entrepreneur had obviously realised that all those new apartments would in time develop dripping taps that someone would have to repair.

Earlier, as the teacher and I sat on the bus for Heng Mountain waiting for it to leave, I'd been drawn to another scene that had given me a glimpse of what change means in China. A scruffy-looking man selling corn-on-the-cob from a bucket boarded to look for customers. There was only a smattering of passengers and no one was buying, but the smell obviously gave one young family an idea. As soon as the street seller left, the two well-dressed parents got off with their little girl and dashed away. They reappeared a few minutes later holding a takeout bag from a nearby McDonald's restaurant. I was surprised to see they'd bought a small tub of corn. They could have saved their energy, and some money, by buying the exact same snack that had just been offered to them at their seats, but being slightly better off they probably thought they could afford to buy something that more accurately reflected their aspirations. Corn from a bucket sold by a shabby hawker is yesterday's China; a Western fast food restaurant is the future.

These thoughts tumbled through my head as we pulled into the small town at the foot of Heng Mountain. The most pressing task was to find a hotel to spend the night. We walked up and down the main street for a little while before a woman approached clutching a pamphlet. She asked if we were looking for somewhere to stay and showed us the booklet in her hand, which advertised rooms for rent in her home. It was halfway up the sacred mountain and inside the park that surrounds it. Nestled in the shade of a wood, it looked an inviting prospect, but the teacher was wary of being overcharged. He motioned for me not to appear too keen so I hung back and let them haggle over the price. Eventually, they struck a deal. Our lodgings were several miles away and up a mountain, so the next question was how we were going to get there. 'Don't worry, my husband has transport,' said the woman, so we shuffled to one side and waited while she made a call on her mobile phone.

Within a few minutes the husband arrived. He virtually crashed his motorbike onto the pavement before swinging his leg theatrically off his machine, like a cowboy dismounting a horse. He held a cigarette loosely between his lips and carried the unmistakable smell of *baijiu*, the ferociously strong Chinese spirit made from rice. It was the middle of the afternoon and I couldn't help thinking that he'd probably been up all night drinking, smoking and playing cards. The woman had obviously not prepared her husband for the load he was expected to carry up the mountain because he took a long look at the teacher, his head moving from top to bottom and then back up again. It was probably the first time he'd been asked to transport a Chinese pensioner dressed as a woman and his younger Western friend. There was a slight pause before he finally spoke, urging us to 'get on'.

It wasn't immediately clear what he wanted us to get on to; there wasn't enough room for three of us and our luggage on his motorbike, but then the woman pointed to her own moped parked nearby. The teacher was to ride behind the husband; I was to sit behind his wife. In China it's impossible for a Westerner with a white face to travel incognito. There's too much physical difference from the rest of the population. I'd once tried to convince a Chinese woman that I was from the western region of Xinjiang, whose original inhabitants look more Turkish than Chinese. I thought my brown hair, darkish complexion and blue eyes made that claim just plausible, but she didn't believe me. So like many foreigners, I'd become accustomed to being pointed at and talked about and not being able to merge into a crowd. There are some occasions though when we draw even more attention to ourselves, and this was definitely one of those times.

After hitching up his tight white trousers, the teacher

gingerly mounted the husband's motorbike. He placed his small suitcase awkwardly between him and the husband before they sped off. I put my rucksack on my back and sat behind the woman. I was just starting to worry about the dangerous weight imbalance when we too roared away. Ahead, I could see the teacher desperately trying to get a better grip on his bag as they ploughed on up the hill. I caught occasional glimpses of light-blue eyeshadow as his head swivelled from side to side. I wondered what a local, perhaps out for a stroll that Saturday afternoon, would have made of the scene, as the two motorbikes and their unusual cargoes flashed by.

Before I went to China I had a mental image of what the country would look like. That picture had mostly come from scenes on china cups and painted scrolls, so was at least a few centuries out of date. The visions I conjured up invariably involved high mountains shrouded in clouds that towered above pastoral scenes of perfect harmony. In my mind's eye, an old man with a long wispy beard might be fishing in the shadow of a pagoda, with a pot of tea placed on a table by his side. A willow tree seemed always to be blowing gently in the breeze somewhere nearby and the fisherman would be unconcerned if he caught nothing all day, it was irrelevant to his overall happiness. The mere act of graceful living was satisfying enough.

Unsurprisingly, the real China rarely lived up to those expectations. I lived in Beijing, a big, ugly concrete metropolis that has drifted a good distance away from the ancient Chinese vision of the perfect place to live. I'd often been struck by how the city's urban vistas are in fact twisted versions of the ones on those ancient Chinese scrolls. The straight, high mountains have been replaced by tower blocks, and the painted white clouds that float gently through the sky have been transformed into oppressive banks of smog, which much of the time hang like damp wads of cotton wool over the Chinese capital. But there are still places in China that have tried to preserve something of that ancient vision, and Heng Mountain is one of them.

When we awoke the following morning in our mountainside idyll, I could smell fresh air and breakfast being cooked down below. Having spent most of my time in China in cities, I rarely heard the chirping of birds, but now that pleasant noise drifted into my room through poorly fitted windows. Below, a travelling butcher had pushed his bicycle up to the house. I looked down and saw pork ribs poking out of a filthy basket attached to the front of the bike. The intestines of some animal, probably a pig, were being carried in a plastic bag hung casually on the handlebars. The butcher was wearing a dirty apron, on which he constantly wiped a large knife and a grubby pair of hands. I was just thinking that I wouldn't like to eat any of the meat he was selling when I remembered the delicious food the homeowner had rustled up the previous evening. I decided not to look any more as the butcher handed over what would probably be that evening's meal.

I wanted to walk up the mountain's beautiful pine-clad slopes, which are dotted with walkways and temples, so I put on my shorts and boots. The teacher though had decided the day was made for dressing up and wore high heels and pink sunglasses with large silver hinges. He'd also fished out of his luggage a jade bracelet and a ring made from the same green stone. He was not kitted out for hiking, so over breakfast we decided he would take the bus to the top of the mountain and wait for me there. I would make my way up on foot.

I was still getting used to the teacher's feminine mode of dress, partly because it sometimes seemed to jar with his masculine movements. One example came just after we'd decided what we were doing. As I sat in the morning sun, the teacher, a reasonably fit pensioner, entertained himself by chasing a chicken around the courtyard of the house we were staying in. His movements were those of a man, but they were accompanied by the sound of his substantial high heels clacking on the stone floor. I wanted to laugh out loud; it was such an amusing scene. I was still a little embarrassed by what the teacher was wearing, but a new feeling was also starting to emerge: pride. I felt honoured that he could finally be himself around me, and happy that he could be open about who he really was in at least some parts of China.

No outdoor endeavour is pursued with such enthusiasm in China as walking up a hill and as I slowly climbed the winding path I kept coming across groups of giggling young people. Many of them were clutching plastic bags containing their lunch. They would stop at temples, half hidden in knolls of trees, to light joss sticks and eat. The experience of walking in China is far more relaxed than in the West, where hikers usually don hard-wearing outdoor clothes and seek out wilder places. In China, paths to the tops of mountains are usually paved and walkers tend to dress as though they are out for a gentle Sunday amble. Many of the women I came across were wearing high-heeled shoes and summer dresses; men were equally smart. Walking in China is also a communal activity. I kept passing groups of people wearing the same coloured bibs with the words 'Heng Mountain pilgrimage' written across the front. Some visitors, like the teacher, decided they didn't want to walk, so were ferried up and down by a fleet of small buses. The screech of brakes as these vehicles hurtled down the mountain was as frequent as the birdsong.

Heng Mountain is unusual in that it celebrates two different ideas: Buddhism and Daoism. There are temples to both creeds strung out across the hillsides. The coexistence of these different belief systems in just one place is another example of that ancient Chinese trait I'd had a hint of while visiting Mao's hometown: the ability to see the appeal of two contradictory ideas at the same time. If Chairman Mao and his rival Liu Shaoqi could come together in a single tour, Buddhism and Daoism could certainly share the same mountain. The ruling communist party must have drawn on this ability to accommodate contrasting ideas when in the 1980s it was forced to say why it was ditching communism in favour of capitalist economic reforms. Party leaders eventually hit upon the term 'socialism with Chinese characteristics' to explain the policy shift. It's a piece of linguistic gymnastics that allows China's rulers to define just about anything they do as socialist. This doublespeak enables the party to claim it hasn't really changed, it's just adapted. It also gives the country's leaders legitimacy and suggests continuity. The use of the term 'Chinese characteristics' is clever in that it implies the leadership's actions are natural and suited to the conditions of China, as though they are merely doing what everyone else would do if they were in power.

There wasn't much communist ideology on show on Heng Mountain. Visitors are mostly confronted with the past, not the present. As I made my way up, I came across a small Daoist temple with a monk inside dressed in Ming dynasty-style clothing. He was wearing a neat blue cotton top with matching trousers. His hair was tied in a bun at the top of his head and he had a short beard. The only personal items that placed him in the twenty-first century were a knitted sweater underneath his outer garments and a pair of designer glasses. He told me he was forty-two and had been living in White Mountain Temple for three years. Chinese government officials are forever telling foreign journalists that they don't understand China and so produce news reports that are inaccurate, biased or misguided. It's a very difficult argument to counter because this criticism contains some truth.

China does have a lot of history and is sometimes difficult to understand, so I was always keen to learn as much as possible from whatever opportunity presented itself. Now I had a Daoist monk in front of me.

Daoism is not an easy concept to get to grips with; it's not even an easy idea to label. It's part religion, part moral code and part folklore. Its origins date back to an ancient sage called Laozi, who was supposed to have been a contemporary of Confucius, but no one's really sure. He might have lived several centuries after Confucius and it's not even certain that he existed at all. Old paintings that depict Laozi often show him wearing a flowing robe, with a bun of hair neatly tied to the top of his head, like the monk I encountered on Heng Mountain, although to the best of my knowledge Laozi did not wear designer glasses. The philosopher's teachings deal with the roguish elements of human nature. Confucius tried to bring order to Chinese society by explaining how the individuals within it are supposed to act, but Laozi was something of a rebel. Confucius wanted sons to obey their fathers, but Laozi might recommend they turn their back on society and wander around barefoot with dishevelled hair. Laozi believed that doing nothing and acting stupid is sometimes the best course of action. It appears to be an acknowledgement that for a successful and fulfilling life people shouldn't always abide by the rules or act appropriately all of the time.

The monk on Heng Mountain appeared to have adopted some of this devil-may-care attitude. He had given up his job and gone to live in a temple on the side of a mountain. His hair was long and greasy, but he didn't seem to mind. He told me he wasn't supposed to cut it because it was a gift from his parents. When I pointed out that his beard seemed to have been trimmed in contravention of this code, he had the perfect Daoist answer: 'I don't find it easy to talk with hair hanging from my chin,' he said with a smile. As we chatted,

I realised I knew another man who also seemed to have a Daoist frame of mind: the teacher. Anyone who could defy convention by dressing in women's clothes could certainly be said to have an irreverent, non-conformist attitude. He often did what he wanted, regardless of what people around him thought.

When I got near the top I saw the teacher sitting on a stone bench waiting for me. Since we'd parted that morning he'd acquired a pink parasol and a yellow wild flower, both of which were peeping out of the top of his handbag. He'd brought along a portable radio and was listening to traditional Chinese music, and singing along. There were hundreds of people milling around, but no one seemed to notice the teacher. He sat there looking like he didn't have a care in the world. He was more relaxed than I'd ever seen before, and when I sat next to him he began talking about the first time he realised he liked wearing women's clothes.

He started putting on his mother's stockings when he was still a small child, at an age when no one saw it as odd. He liked the way they felt on his skin and continued raiding her wardrobe throughout his childhood. He was often jealous of his sister, who was bought far more colourful clothes than he was ever allowed to wear. At university, the teacher used to put on women's underwear under his dull student's garb, but by that age and in that time of conformity he knew he was doing something that would be difficult to explain, even to his closest friends. 'I felt very alone,' he said. It wasn't until the turn of the century that the teacher realised China had thousands of people – probably many more – who liked cross-dressing. It was only from that moment, when he was nearly fifty years old, that he began to have the confidence to explore who he really was.

The teacher's life was changed by the internet. As soon as he got online he started to search for people like him and to his great relief he found them. On one memorable occasion he agreed to meet another cross-dresser, just to prove to himself that they were real people and not just online identities. The teacher said he'd never felt so happy as when he saw the other man had turned up and, more importantly, was dressed as a woman. At the time the teacher was still shy about expressing his feelings and so he walked away without speaking to the man, but he now knew for sure that there were other people like him.

The teacher is now mostly comfortable with who he is. When we were together he never appeared embarrassed about wearing women's clothes and never hid himself away. But it had not been easy to get to that point. As we sat on Heng Mountain he told me about the first time he walked through the streets of Beijing dressed as a woman. It happened one night when he'd gone to a friend's home. The friend, also a cross-dresser, knew the teacher would never go out in public on his own without a little coaxing, so he pushed him out of the door and shut it behind him. From inside the flat he told the teacher to walk around and not to come back for ten minutes. 'My cheeks were burning red,' he told me, 'but I did it.'

There are still times when the teacher hesitates to wear women's clothes or tones down his outfit. Later on, I realised the extent to which he showed his feminine side depended on how far he was from Beijing and his established life in the capital. Sat on Heng Mountain, surrounded by people he didn't know and who didn't know him, he felt free to be who he wanted to be, but in Beijing he was far more cautious. He might wear a spangly T-shirt or a piece of delicate jewellery, but his other life as a cross-dresser was never obvious. That's why I'd seen the signs but not understood them. The teacher talked about this problem. 'Some people understand, others don't,' was how he put it. He said the wife of one friend was very helpful. She'd taught him how to put on make-up and they often go shopping together, but other people are less accepting and so in front of them he appears as they expect him to appear: dressed as a man. In Beijing there's also the problem of bumping into someone unexpectedly, perhaps a former colleague or a childhood friend who doesn't know his secret. The teacher said his car had helped solve that difficulty. Cocooned in his own private space, he can travel wherever he wants dressed however he wants, with little fear of seeing someone who might recognise him.

I initially thought the teacher's cross-dressing was perhaps another example of how foreign influences were making people more individualistic in China, giving them the opportunity to express themselves properly for the first time. Then I read more about cross-dressing itself and realised that it has far deeper roots. The act of wearing clothing or accessories usually associated with the opposite sex has a long history. It's been a feature of many different societies in many different ages. For centuries, both men and women have cross-dressed to express themselves, for comfort or out of necessity. Why should China be any different?

In some ways, traditional Chinese culture is perfectly suited to cross-dressing. It offers few objections to different kinds of sexual orientation or gender expression. The West's Christian tradition means some people still see homosexuals, lesbians and transgender people as sinful, but in China there's no strong religious challenge to those who deviate from the norm. Confucianism, Daoism and Buddhism are largely silent on these issues. As I've mentioned before, there's always been great pressure on Chinese people to produce children, but as long as that obligation was fulfilled there was often a tolerance shown towards people's private lives. In many eras they could do whatever they wanted if they kept it to themselves. In the Ming and Qing dynasties it was fashionable for those drawn from higher social classes to engage in homosexual relationships.

There's little evidence of the extent of cross-dressing under the emperors, but it's not unreasonable to assume it went on because we know the concept existed. Gender disguise, for example, is a recurring theme in storytelling about cross-dressing, and China has its own story based around this idea: Mulan. The story was popularised by Disney, but it's based on an ancient Chinese ballad in which a young woman dresses as a man to join the army. The ballad tells how each family has to send someone to defend China against an invading force. Mulan's father is old and weak and her brother just a child, so this young woman – already trained in martial arts, sword fighting and archery – decides to go herself. She apparently kept her gender a secret for 12 years. It's difficult to imagine the idea for the ballad simply springing from nowhere. Cross-dressing must surely have existed.

Cross-dressing is also an established part of Chinese opera. The origins date back to a time when there were all-male or all-female theatrical troupes, so obviously men had to play women and women had to play men, but the tradition carried on long after there were joint productions. It's not entirely clear why it continued when it didn't have to, but the fascination with cross-dressing appears to have been a factor. One critic explained that many theatre-goers in the 1920s and 30s, a golden age for Chinese opera, found it more interesting to watch a man play a woman, and master graceful feminine traits, than watch a woman do the same thing. This cross-dressing would occasionally produce some complicated storylines, which audiences also seemed to appreciate. A male actor taking the role of Mulan would mean a man playing a young woman who was pretending to be a young man in order to fight on behalf of her father.

Not everyone in China enjoyed opera's cross-dressing

tradition. The Chinese author Lu Xun, who wrote in the first half of the twentieth century, thought it reflected the corruption and ruin of the old order. He wanted a new China that was, as he termed it, strong and masculine, not weak and feminine. At the time he was writing, one of China's greatest-ever opera stars, a man called Mei Lanfang, was popularising this art form across the world. He befriended Hollywood stars and toured Europe, where his feminine appearance and refined voice found appreciative audiences. 'China's greatest, most eternal and universal "art" is man playing woman,' grumbled Lu Xun.

During the Cultural Revolution traditional Chinese opera was banned, to be replaced by eight model operas promoted by Chairman Mao's wife, Jiang Qing. These focused on issues such as class struggle and the fight against Japan during the Second World War, instead of more ancient themes and stories. Opera troupes were disbanded and actors and writers persecuted, like so many others. The Cultural Revolution politicised many aspects of life, not just art. Sex and gender became public as well as private issues. Just think of Liu Shaoqi's wife being paraded in a *qipao* and fake pearls. It was a bad time to be gay or a cross-dresser, although strangely the clothing worn during the Cultural Revolution blurred the line between male and female. Men and women dressed in almost identical outfits. The few colours available – blue, green and grey – were repeated for both sexes, as were the patterns. Nearly everyone wore simple, military-style cuts. A man and his wife could have switched clothes without drawing anyone's attention.

The pressure to conform in the Cultural Revolution was enormous, so it's no surprise that people kept their individuality under wraps. No one celebrated being different. That slowly began to change when China started to open up to the outside world under Deng Xiaoping, but by that time

Chinese people seemed to have forgotten their own history of same-sex desire, cross-dressing and gender diversity. Sexual and gender differences were seen as an import from the West, and not always a welcome one.

In the early 1980s, party leaders were so worried that unwanted Western influences would change the character of their people that they launched something called the Anti-Spiritual Pollution Campaign. It was directed at all kinds of dangerous ideas, including individualism, which the communists thought might undermine China's collectivist outlook. Inevitably, it was difficult to work out exactly which ideas were beneficial to China's development and which would undermine the fabric of society, and so the campaign was interpreted in a number of different ways. For some officials it became an attack on what was seen as the excesses and vulgarity of the West. In his book *Red Dust*, the author Ma Jian describes how the launch of this campaign convinced him to leave Beijing. He wore denim and had long hair and his boss criticised him for having a lax, free-wheeling attitude towards life. At the time, these kinds of accusations were dangerous and might result in a spell in prison. I remember the teacher once told me that he wouldn't have dared dress as a woman in public in the 1980s. Times have changed. Most people in China now have a far broader view of what is acceptable.

The teacher never seemed worried about getting into trouble with the police because of his choice of clothing. Maybe that's because by the time I knew him he'd been dressing as a woman in public for many years without attracting their attention. Later on, when I tried to find out what the law had to say on this issue, I found it hard to work out whether or not he was breaking any rules. China's legal system says little about cross-dressing. What is clear is that people who are different have not always been afforded proper legal protection. Homosexuals were given greater legal freedom only in 1997 when China revised its legal code and removed the crime of 'hooliganism', which until then had been used to harass gay men. Homosexuality though remained on the list of official mental disorders for four more years. The legal status of lesbian, gay, bisexual and transgender people can perhaps best be summed up by the Chinese phrase: don't encourage, don't discourage, don't promote – but that still leaves people open to discrimination. While the law might not ban cross-dressing, it doesn't seem to protect it much either. That wasn't too much of a problem for the teacher. He was already retired and didn't have to answer to a boss, but it would have been a different matter had he wanted to protect his right to go to work wearing women's clothing.

As with many other issues in China, it's only partially useful to examine the law when trying to work out the legality of cross-dressing. In China, the legal system is more flexible than in other countries. Laws that seem clear-cut on paper can take on a vaguer quality in practice. Rules that prohibit certain types of behaviour can be broken and ignored and often no one seems to mind, least of all the police. Similarly, the law might guarantee a particular right that doesn't exist in reality. China's constitution provides many wonderful examples of this phenomenon. Article 35 promises Chinese citizens freedom of speech, freedom of the press and the freedom to demonstrate, but just try holding up a banner criticising the government in Beijing's Tiananmen Square. Count the seconds before the police turn up.

The law is best thought of as an extension of the country's many political campaigns. The communist party gets worried about this or that and instructs the various arms of government, including the police, to sort out the problem. Whenever there was a major international event in Beijing, meaning lots of media attention on the Chinese capital, the authorities would close down all the shops and stalls that sold fake DVDs. It was an inconvenience for people who lived in the capital and wanted to watch the latest films, but we knew that as soon as the foreign dignitaries left town, counterfeit movies would once again be available. The law relating to illegal DVDs must have remained constant, but the police were only interested in enforcing it when it became politically necessary to do so. The teacher had obviously sensed which way the wind was blowing when it came to cross-dressing. He knew the authorities had too many other things on their plate without bothering about men who wanted to wear women's clothes. It didn't matter what the law might say.

A much more pressing problem for the teacher was how his family viewed his cross-dressing. It was a sensitive subject and one I mostly steered clear of. I noticed that whenever I spoke to the teacher about his wife while he was dressed as a woman he would be less open than usual. It was often difficult to stop him talking, but on these occasions he seemed to have little to say and would respond to my questions with one-word answers. He told me that his wife knew about his love of women's clothes, but didn't really approve. She tolerated it and the teacher seemed to know where the boundaries were. Whenever I saw them together he was never dressed as a woman. His son was an even trickier issue. Like most fathers, the teacher loves his child dearly. I enjoyed listening to him talk about his son because he spoke with such affection. They argued about the usual family issues, about what job the young man would do and how much money the teacher was willing to give him to buy a car, but they got on well. I didn't like to talk about what his son knew about his cross-dressing because I sensed the teacher was still grappling with this complicated subject himself.

He did once speak about his love of women's clothing in relation to his son. It was while we were idling away a few hours in a coffee shop in Qiqihar, that dull city in Heilongjiang province. The teacher had on a long black wig, a bejewelled white top and bright pink lipstick. He looked relaxed and comfortable and happy, but then he surprised me by saying he hoped his son didn't turn out like him. At first I thought it was a slightly odd thing to say. The teacher had spent years suppressing his feelings and was relieved those years were now behind him. Surely, I thought, the lesson to be drawn from those experiences was that every individual is different? Surely, those differences must be celebrated and encouraged and not hidden away? Then I reminded myself that not everyone likes other people to be different and a cross-dresser in China, as in many other parts of the world, still faces prejudice, despite rapidly changing attitudes. The teacher's hope that his own son would not wear women's clothes seemed to me an acknowledgement that life for people who are different can often be difficult. He wanted his son's life to be as smooth and trouble free as possible.

It was getting chilly on Heng Mountain so we finished talking and decided to walk to the very top. It wasn't far, but even this distance proved too much for some. The sedan chair is making a comeback in China and a few tourists were being carried the last leg of the journey on the shoulders of others. Several large people sat in what looked like ordinary dining room chairs that had been lashed to two poles. It was a hot day and the pole bearers were working hard. Sweat was dripping down their faces and occasionally, with the poles resting on their shoulders, they'd stop to wipe it away with a flannel brought along for that very purpose. It was just a small example of how the communist ideal of equality is slowly being chipped away in China. Some people are carried and others do the carrying. I thought this was perhaps another example of 'socialism with Chinese characteristics'.

At the top of the mountain, people crowded into a small

temple to pray. They put their hands together and touched them to their foreheads, before bending to their knees and repeating the process. Some read prayers from yellow scrolls of paper, others burned incense. Off to one side, I saw a woman shake a holder that contained several short sticks. She let them fall to the floor and then looked closely at the pattern they had formed, hoping to divine her future from what seemed like a random array of wood. The teacher and I then did what we'd gone to Heng Mountain to do. We walked to the edge of the cliff and peered over. I gasped at the scene that lay below. I was looking at something that I'd first seen on those china cups, from which the elderly people of my childhood had drunk tea. The peaks stretched into the distance, pushing up from lush green valleys. The clouds hung over the mountain tops or swooped around them. People stood and stared as the wind blew in their ears. Back at the bottom of the mountain, right next to the entrance to the park, there's a sign that tries to sum up the beauty of Heng Mountain. In badly written English it says:

> The drifting clouds among the peaks resemble rosefinches on wings, while the running mountain springs with white cascading waterfalls look like snow falling in summer; sounds like thunders booming from the blue.

I'd wondered about those lines when I spotted them the day before as I entered the park. From my time working as a sub-editor on the *China Daily*, I knew that Chinese writers can sometimes be guilty of exaggeration and often use flowery language. But as I stood at the top of the mountain looking down I could see what the author of those awkward words had meant. The writer hadn't done such a bad job of trying to describe the beauty of Heng Mountain.

The Art Of Propaganda

By his own admission, the teacher wasn't the most energetic of people and he didn't always make the most of opportunities when they presented themselves. Fortunately, he's not a man who has many regrets, and he's more likely to laugh than cry at past errors. Still, even he had to draw deep on his reserves of sangfroid when he missed an appointment with the president of China. Readers might wonder how the teacher's life had suddenly jumped from mundane shifts making monosodium glutamate to appointments with China's top leader. It was a dizzying change and caught the teacher off-guard too.

He finished his university course in 1987 and, as had been agreed, went back to the factory. He'd glimpsed other possibilities though and so wasn't satisfied in his old job. As before, he was desperate to leave, but he now had a university degree and so escape was a real possibility. He wanted a job that would allow him to write and was overjoyed when a friend found him one in the propaganda department of a giant Beijing food company. It was 1990, the start of a new decade and the start of a new life for the teacher. Work wasn't the only thing that was changing. The teacher now had a wife. He was nearly forty, late to be getting married in China, but the Cultural Revolution had disrupted more than just people's education; every aspect of their lives had been put on hold as China's leaders turned society on its head.

The food company was state owned and ran factories, processing plants and shops. It had thousands of workers and the teacher's job was to head a small department primarily responsible for producing the firm's fortnightly newspaper. His appointment with the Chinese president, a position held at the time by Jiang Zemin, came a few years into his job, when the leader of China decided to visit one of the company's shops. It was a prestigious occasion and a rare opportunity for the firm to bask in the reflected glory of a man who led more than one billion people.

The teacher was charged with recording the president's visit for the in-house newspaper. Writing copy about a politician's visit to a shop selling daily necessities is not usually the basis for literary fame, but it was certainly a step up from the factory floor and it would give the teacher the chance to show off his skills. Unfortunately, he was late for the most important task he'd so far undertaken in his working life. Security around the president was understandably tight and the teacher, like everyone else, had been told to be in the shop by 6am. When he turned up two hours after the appointed hour, Mr Jiang's security detail refused to let him in. The teacher usually manages to talk his way out of, or into, all kinds of situations, but getting them to change their minds was, not surprisingly, beyond him.

However, like all good reporters he didn't panic. The teacher was beginning to have confidence in his own ability to sort out a problem. He knew he would be able to talk to people inside the shop after the president had left, to find out what he had said and which company product had caught his eye, but the teacher didn't have a photograph. He'd gone to the meeting armed with his own camera, but hadn't got anywhere near Mr Jiang. He finally contacted a photographer who'd attended the event for China's main state-run news agency, Xinhua. The snapper was willing to send the teacher three shots, but China was now beginning to embrace market economics and he demanded 100 yuan (£10) for each frame. The teacher agreed and asked for a receipt to claim back the money. No receipt, said the photographer, who was obviously hoping to keep the extra cash for himself. The teacher had no choice but to agree. He then used a little creative accounting to claim the money back from elsewhere. He had his report, he had his photographs – and he wasn't out of pocket.

When the teacher spoke about his time in the propaganda department, he often told stories that made it clear just how many opportunities for corruption are presented to even lowly officials in China. One particular story sticks out because it was so ordinary. The teacher's company ran a restaurant that specialised in the spicy cuisine of Hunan, Chairman Mao's home province. Unfortunately, customers were scarce and the teacher was given the task of drumming up business. Part of his job involved dealing with journalists who wanted to do stories about his company, so the teacher had a full contacts book and had no trouble persuading a famous reporter to visit the restaurant to try its food.

Just in case the journalist misunderstood what was being asked of him, he was given a red envelope for his trouble, with 1,000 yuan (about £100) stuffed inside. These envelopes, known as *hong bao*, are often given to Chinese reporters when they cover an event. *Hong bao* also smooth the way for millions of other daily interactions. They ensure a doctor gives a patient the best treatment possible and help a parent secure a place for their child at a good school. Not surprisingly, the journalist hired by the teacher produced a glowing report about the restaurant's superlative offerings. Customers flooded the place and for years afterwards the teacher would regularly receive calls from the grateful manager, inviting him there to dine. 'What for?' the teacher would ask. 'No reason,' the manager would reply. Of course there was a reason, it's just no one wanted to say it out loud. The teacher had once done the man a big favour and was getting his reward. Stories like this are so commonplace that many Chinese people simply brush them aside; not so much corruption as a perk of the job.

The teacher's quick mind, and even quicker tongue, meant he was perfectly suited to the demands of his job. He was a conduit for information, using his articles to pass news to the company's workers and his eyes and ears to report back to his bosses. The department was plugged into a wider propaganda network. The teacher's team were responsible for promoting political campaigns launched by the communist-controlled government. When he retired he discovered that one of his colleagues had been spying on everyone at the firm for the country's internal security machine. She would relay information about what people were saying and who was politically reliable.

The job also gave the teacher a little power. Managers of the firm's various branches and departments would clamour to appear in the company newspaper, as a favourable article could help them gain promotion. They would sometimes offer tempting gifts to persuade the teacher to put their names in print; it might be a watch, an expensive bottle of liquor or a carton of cigarettes. The teacher said he never accepted any of these presents, but I'm not sure I believe him. It would have taken superhuman restraint to turn down everything and he didn't seem like a man who could resist temptation forever, or even for a short time. Giving gifts is also an established part of life in China, so to continually refuse to accept a present might have put him out of step with his colleagues.

I was interested in hearing about the teacher's job because propaganda is one way in which the communist party maintains tight control over its people. All politicians like to spin a story to show themselves in the best possible light, but the practice is more developed in China. There are clear channels of information between ruler and ruled, and alternative viewpoints that might interfere with the party line are blocked. Propaganda is the means by which China's leaders put across their message and make sure everyone falls into line. I don't remember ever driving through a Chinese village without seeing some slogan or other painted on a wall or on a banner strung across the main street. Most of these slogans would urge people to abide by China's strict family planning rules, when they were still in place. Some would even threaten sterilisation or financial ruin if couples had more children than were allowed. Whatever the subject, these bite-sized pieces of propaganda were always there; cajoling, reminding and informing people who might otherwise forget what the party was doing for them.

Propaganda is so important that even the lowest levels of government employ people dedicated to the task. Even the teacher's food company felt the need to spread the right message, so it's no surprise that Chinese officials are forever on the lookout for a good way to promote what they do. Even an everyday wedding in a forgotten corner of rural China can be shaped into a morality tale that shows the benevolence of the communist party.

I came across the story of the wedding by chance. I'd travelled with some colleagues to the banks of a massive reservoir called Danjiangkou, which straddles the provinces of Henan and Hubei. The reservoir was about to be expanded as part of an ambitious engineering project called the South-to-North Water Diversion Project. The clue to the purpose of the scheme is in the name: it diverts water from the wet south to the dry north through a system of canals, pipes and pumping stations. The scale of the project is immense, second only to the building of the Three Gorges

Dam on the Yangtze River. Chinese leaders have never been short of ambition and their plan to solve the north's water shortage was nothing short of staggering. Danjiangkou is at the southern end of the project and is where much of the water is held before being sent north.

When I visited, tens of thousands of people lived around the reservoir and the first part of the scheme would require many of them to move. In most countries such an undertaking would be impossible. Leaving aside the organisational difficulties of relocating so many people, the authorities would simply not be able to persuade them to leave their homes, and disputes would take years to wind their way through the law courts. If that wasn't enough, dislodging settled residents from around Danjiangkou seemed particularly difficult: the fertile soil grows oranges, providing the farmers who live there with incomes that they might not be able to earn elsewhere. But this was China, and if the country's leaders decided to move a mountain, they moved a mountain. In the end people had no choice. A message printed on a banner tied across a street in the village of Guanmenyan, on the edge of the reservoir, summed up the mood: 'Whether you go earlier or later, you'll all have to move.'

Even though they had to go, people still grumbled about the upheaval and so local officials had to coax them out of their homes. They tried appealing to people's better natures, emphasising the national importance of the scheme and reminding residents that the good of society had to be put before any individual need. That kind of talk only gets you so far, so the government also tried money. In theory, people were handsomely compensated for uprooting their lives. Officials promised new homes, fertile land and plenty of leisure time in the distant regions these internal migrants were being sent to. They tried to convince them that it was not just a new start, but also that a better life awaited them.

Local bureaucrats used propaganda to stress the benefits of moving. That's why officials seized upon the marriage of a young man called Ding Guanyan.

Mr Ding had originally lived in Guanmenyan, but the planned reservoir expansion had already forced him and his parents, along with other family members, to move to a new home several hours' drive away, near the city of Zaoyang. That's where I'd stumbled upon them, when I travelled to the area to see how people who'd already been moved were getting on. After just a few months in his new home, Mr Ding had met and fallen in love with a local woman. The couple became engaged and then married. The event was good news for the family, but also an opportunity for the local propaganda department, which wanted to underline the benefits of moving. What better way to do that than to hold out the prospect of love for some of those who migrated? An article about the wedding appeared in a provincial newspaper and was soon afterwards picked up by the national media. In one report there were photographs of the happy couple celebrating Chinese New Year under the catchy headline: move to a new house; marry a new bride; enjoy a new year. There was also a comment from a local politician, who claimed the wedding was proof of how well the new arrivals were settling in. The article boasted about the new homes built for the migrants, the factories for them to work in and the schools where their children could learn. There were paved roads, facilities for gas heating and pipes for running water. What could be better?

Unfortunately for the migrants, the reality was rather different. Mr Ding's family had farmed oranges back in Guanmenyan, but in their new home were forced to grow less profitable wheat. The family income had plummeted and they longed to be back by the waters of Danjiangkou. The family's financial situation was so bad that Mr Ding and his elder brother were thinking of moving to one of China's booming coastal cities to find work. As I chatted to them in their new home, they also started grumbling about corruption. They said they had not seen all the money that had been set aside for their move; some of it, they said, had been diverted into the pockets of officials who were in charge of the process. They wondered aloud whether legal action would help them get more.

It was at this point that a delegation of police officers and local officials suddenly walked into the house. It was as if they'd been waiting for the conversation to take on a darker tone before deciding to put in an appearance. They didn't bother knocking, but simply sauntered in and uttered a few half-hearted apologies, demanding to see my identity card. No one in the family complained; people rarely do in such situations in China. The head of the delegation explained that they were simply there to observe, but the Ding family instantly became more cautious. A little later when the bride-groom's mother was showing me and my colleague around her new house, she quietly closed a door and started talking in a whisper. 'Those are the people who took our money,' she said, meaning the officials still occupying her living room downstairs. 'They don't want us to talk to you.' The Ding family had certainly been settled into a new life, but not everything could be said to be going well. The news reports about the wedding were part of a carefully orchestrated propaganda campaign that had told only part of a story, and not all of the rest was worth celebrating.

I didn't know the marriage had been used as a propaganda tool until some way into my conversation with the Dings, but I knew there'd been a wedding in the family almost as soon as I stepped over their threshold. It was impossible not to spot the giant photograph of the newlyweds that had pride of place in the new home. It was the most colourful item in a house that still had bare concrete walls. In the picture, Mr Ding leans over his sitting bride. His hair looks slick and is parted at one side. He's wearing a shirt with frills down the front and a blue jacket with white piping along its edge. His bride is wearing a white, Western-style wedding dress and is sitting on an ornate chair that looks like it's come from the court of an eighteenth-century French king.

Modern Chinese wedding photographs are nearly always very elaborate and very large. Most are taken before the actual day itself, at any romantic spot that can be found in a country that's still going through its industrial revolution. It's not uncommon to see brides and their grooms posing for photographs in parks, outside old colonial buildings or beside fetid lakes.

I couldn't take my eyes off Mr Ding's wedding photo. Its mere cheerfulness seemed so out of place in what was a drab community, whose members were still coming to terms with the upheaval of their lives. The whole place had been recently built to house the new migrants and there were still half-finished buildings dotted around, suggesting lives not yet fully put back together. It reminded me more of an open prison than somewhere I might want to live, but the wedding photograph suggested the Dings were looking forward to a brighter future. Local officials had hijacked the marriage, but it had still been a genuinely joyous event.

The story of how a real event had been spun into something far more meaningful reminded me of Lei Feng, the Chinese soldier whose life had been turned into the most famous propaganda campaign of them all. The teacher had grown up with these stories and often talked about Lei Feng. Most of the time he was being ironic, laughing at the ridiculousness of the tales, but not always. When you hear something so many times, fact and fiction begin to merge. It's not certain that someone called Lei Feng ever existed in the way he's portrayed but his life story, and his supposed devotion to the communist party and the people of China, has for decades been held up as an example for others to follow. It still is. In 1963 Mao himself urged people to learn from Comrade Lei Feng, guaranteeing the young man eternal fame. A photograph of the soldier wearing a warm winter hat, with side flaps dangling down like big, floppy ears, is still one of the most recognisable images in China.

Lei Feng's story reads like a fairy tale. He was supposedly born in 1940 into a poor family, at a time when much of China was under Japanese occupation. Communist history relates how Lei Feng's father was beaten by Japanese soldiers and died in 1945. A year later his brother was dead, aged just twelve. He'd contracted tuberculosis while working in a factory and his mother was so poor she couldn't afford medicine to treat him. Later, Lei Feng's younger brother died and then in a final blow his mother hanged herself after being 'dishonoured' by a local landlord. Lei Feng was just seven and would have been forgiven if he'd been unable to overcome the traumatic events that had already engulfed his family. If the story is to be believed though, he managed to remain cheerful.

Lei Feng went to live with an uncle and threw himself into his schoolwork, but he gave it all up at sixteen to go and work on a farm when the call went out for young volunteers. Communist China was then just a few years old and many people genuinely believed they were building a new civilisation. Even by the standards of the time, Lei Feng would have stood out as an extraordinary character. Take the story of a trip he once made into town to buy some new clothes. When he saw a group of people asking for donations to help buy tractors for a new state-run farm, he apparently didn't hesitate to hand over the money he'd saved for himself. Another story tells of how he would stay behind after meetings to tidy up and make a fire, to ensure the room was clean and warm for the next occupants.

Later, Lei Feng went to work at an iron and steel plant. His meagre belongings fitted into a single small suitcase but, with a harmonica in his pocket, he set off cheerfully to his new workplace on his first-ever train journey. Stories about Lei Feng at the plant become even more unbelievable. He's credited with saving a delivery of cement threatened by rain by covering it with padded coats and quilts. He also apparently prevented another load of cement from going hard by turning it over using just his legs and feet.

At the end of 1959, Lei Feng joined the army and after basic training became a truck driver. Needless to say, his good deeds continued. He apparently mended the socks of fellow soldiers and taught them how to read and write. When he wasn't working he would even collect dung and deliver it to local farmers so they could fertilise their fields. If he had any spare time, he would read Mao's selected works or the famous Soviet novel, *How the Steel Was Tempered*. He also kept a diary and its entries put into words his uniquely selfless attitude towards the people around him.

Like many other heroic lives, Lei Feng's was cut short. One day in August 1962, just after it had stopped raining, one of Lei Feng's comrades attempted to reverse a truck onto open ground so it could be washed. Lei Feng was directing him. Unfortunately, the lorry slipped into a ditch and knocked over a wooden telephone pole, which fell down and struck Lei Feng on the head. Nothing could be done to save the young hero, who was just twenty-one when he died. A crowd of 100,000 is supposed to have turned up to his funeral, to say goodbye to the soldier who always seemed to be smiling. Some of his diary entries had appeared in print during his lifetime, but afterwards they were published more widely, to instruct others on how they should think and act. Since then, the Chinese Communist Party has never tired of promoting the spirit of Lei Feng, and his life has been celebrated in song, dance and film.

Did Lei Feng really exist? There are certainly plenty of photographs of a man the Chinese authorities say was Lei Feng, and the producers of a documentary about the soldier's life interviewed a number of people who said they'd known him. But even if we suspend disbelief and take as fact the extraordinary stories about Lei Feng's good deeds, it's easy to find evidence that, at the very least, his life was exaggerated. Those photographs offer one clue. The lighting and composition suggest a professional photographer took them. Many show Lei Feng performing ordinary tasks; in one he's tinkering with a screwdriver and in another he's washing his truck. Why was a photographer on hand to record the mundane life of a simple soldier? They were taken at a time when China was recovering from the famine that followed the *Great Leap Forward*, so the authorities would have had neither time nor energy to document the life of one soldier, unless the party was already preparing him as a role model for others to follow. Nowadays, every aspect of a person's life can be recorded on the phones in our pockets, but Chinese people were then still decades away from owning cameras.

Lei Feng has become something of a joke in twenty-first-century China because his life seems so out of tune with how people live now. The teacher though was fascinated by him, so when we went to Changsha to see Mao's birthplace he wanted us to make a detour to visit Lei Feng's hometown, which was nearby. The humble house where the soldier is supposed to have spent the first few years of his life has been preserved for curious visitors to wander round. It's a simple brick dwelling with wooden beams and a thatched roof. There's nothing much inside. The house was once in a desperately poor town, but the area has now become a leafy suburb of Changsha. Next to Lei Feng's former home there are expensive villas that offer the possibility of luxurious living. Promotional posters for these new homes suggest Chinese people now aspire to comfortable material lives and not the communist paradise Lei Feng was trying to build. The advertisements seemed to say more about China today than the place where Lei Feng used to live.

One particular advert caught my eye. On it there was a painting of a beautiful European woman in what looked like a dress from the nineteenth century. She was holding a red fan. Next to her was a dapper Western gentleman dressed in a more modern-looking black suit. He was also wearing a top hat and had one hand casually thrust into his pocket, which gave him a relaxed, almost nonchalant, bearing. The two people weren't really standing with each other; the images appeared to have been pulled together from separate sources. Behind them was a horse-drawn carriage and, further back still, there was a faint outline of what appeared to be the Eiffel Tower in Paris. At the top of the poster were the words 'Since England' in English. At first sight, the words and pictures seemed little more than a jumbled mess of thoughts and ideas. What era was it supposed to be? Which European country was the advert showing? What did the English phrase mean? But when I stood back from the poster and looked again I realised that it had successfully conveyed a simple message. It was offering Chinese people with money the chance to live a different and more elegant life, one that foreigners were already enjoying.

As I looked around the area I was struck by another thought: if Lei Feng's family had not died and had somehow managed to hold on to their old home, they would now find themselves the owners of a valuable piece of real estate. They could have sold up and made a fortune. I was pleased with my update of Lei Feng's story, but then a Chinese friend joked that the young soldier's family would not have benefited. He said they would have been kicked off the land by greedy developers in cahoots with the local government. He was probably right. One of the saddest series of stories I covered during my time in China concerned poor people who were thrown out of their homes to make way for redevelopment. These tales were so commonplace that eventually I stopped thinking of them as news.

I was once jolted out of this complacency on a visit to Tongzhou, just outside Beijing. Rapid development has turned what was once a town into a suburb of the capital. I went there to visit a community of people who were being forced from their homes to make way for even more building work. Their story was depressingly all too familiar. Residents said they had been given no choice but to move. They complained that the compensation they were being offered was far too small to allow them to buy another home. Some people had agreed to go and their rickety single-storey houses had already been bulldozed, but others were holding out. The parcel of land on which they lived was a strange mix of flattened earth, where developers had already started work, and an occasional building. These usually stood alone in a sea of empty space. Dwellings like these have long been known as 'nail houses' because they stand out like a nail about to be hammered into a plank of wood. The Chinese character *chai* was painted on walls across the site. It means 'demolish'. You saw it everywhere in China.

I was in a small courtyard chatting to some of the residents who were refusing to go when suddenly a door opened and in stepped a woman who no longer had a recognisable face. She'd been so badly burned that her lips and hair had gone. Her entire face was red and disfigured and she looked in terrible pain. It was shocking to see this woman close up and I instinctively recoiled. She handed me a passport-sized photograph of what she used to look like. I still have it. The picture shows Zhang Shulan in middle age. She was a strong-looking woman with a thick neck and a determined expression. As tears rolled down her face, Mrs Zhang told me her story. It wasn't a long one; she had simply not wanted to leave her home and was angry at the compensation being offered. As in so many other cases in China, she could find no sympathetic ear in authority to listen to her story, so in sheer frustration she set herself alight. 'I didn't want to live. They forced me. I had no choice.' She looked understandably forlorn, probably realising that her act of defiance would not affect the outcome of her battle to save her house. If local officials wanted to redevelop, sooner or later they would redevelop.

Lei Feng's old house had conjured up a series of complicated thoughts and reflections. China was like that. I'd often come across something that initially seemed simple to understand, but then I'd realise it wasn't. Of course, the communist party tries to weed out the contradictions and grey areas of whatever story it's trying to tell in order to present a simple narrative. That's the whole point of propaganda, and a museum dedicated to Lei Feng right next to his former home is a reminder of that fact. The main episodes of the soldier's life are presented in a series of tableaux, where evil-looking Japanese soldiers cower before brave and defiant Chinese peasants. Items from Lei Feng's life are laid out in glass display cases. In one his shoes, watch and leather jacket are on show. In another there's an enamel bowl, a cup and a flannel. Simple objects from a simple life. The aim is obviously to encourage others to follow Lei Feng's example and devote their lives to rebuilding China under the communist party. The message seemed out of date. The latest Apple phone, a home of their own, a satisfying job, foreign travel and the freedom to map out their own lives is far more important to Chinese people now.

I was beginning to wonder if there was anyone who still believed in Lei Feng when the teacher and I came across a young woman standing in the middle of the museum. She was reading out extracts from the model soldier's diary to anyone who would listen. She was twenty and a first-year student at a local university. She told us she came from Shanxi province and this was her first day as a volunteer at the museum. She'd first heard Lei Feng's story as a child and it had so moved her that when she arrived in Changsha she had immediately offered to work at the museum for free.

'Lei Feng is as relevant today as he's always been,' she said with genuine enthusiasm. Giving up her own time seemed proof that she believed what she was saying. It was a reminder that not everything from the past has been discarded. The communist party has reinvented itself since the time of Mao, when it tried to control every aspect of people's lives, even their thoughts. It has now become more sophisticated. It has given people more choices and more freedom, but party leaders still present themselves as the only people capable of leading China into a bright future. They still use crude propaganda campaigns like the one built around Lei Feng to hammer people's thinking into shape, and the student volunteer at the Lei Feng museum shows that message is still getting through.

I was fascinated by the party's ability to use propaganda to get people to believe in its view of the world. Religious organisations do it all the time, but they usually build on solid foundations, on traditions that have been around for centuries. By contrast, when China's communists came to power in 1949 hardly anyone in the country had heard of Marx or Lenin. Despite this handicap, the party was able to convince people in a relatively short space of time that it was right. There were those who doubted the party's wisdom and criticised its policies but they were, at least initially, a minority voice. Most people were willing to give the party a chance to prove itself.

I realised just how potent the communists' propaganda machine had been when I met Robert Ford, a ninety-year-old former British diplomat. Mr Ford was exactly as I imagined a former British diplomat would be: smartly dressed, polite and modest enough to be reluctant to talk about what had been, by anyone's measure, an extraordinary life, much of it spent abroad in the service of the British government. As we chatted in his well-kept London home, with a large expanse of lawn stretching out below the living room window, I couldn't help thinking he was the living embodiment, or at least the popular image, of what it means to be British. Mr Ford though had once been detained by China's communists and on the verge of renouncing everything he stood for. The fact that the Chinese government made good progress in changing the thinking of a man from such a different background reveals just how easy it is to reshape a mind.

Robert Ford had been in the Royal Air Force during the Second World War and when it ended he found himself in India, teaching Indian army officers how to be radio operators. He then got a job as a radio operator at the British mission in Lhasa, the capital of Tibet. He liked it so much that he applied to do a similar job for the Tibetan government. Tibet is now a part of China, something the Chinese government says has been the case for many centuries, but when Mr Ford was there China was going through a civil war and was in no position to enforce its claims to the Himalayan region. Tibetans were largely left to govern themselves. Mr Ford was sent to Chamdo, a town in eastern Tibet, where he was responsible for maintaining radio contact with the central government in Lhasa. Then in 1949 China's civil war ended suddenly with a communist victory, and the following year the party sent a small force into Tibet to reassert its authority. Mr Ford left it too late to escape and was caught by advancing Chinese soldiers. He faced a long list of serious charges, including spying, and was sent to prison for five years. For much of that time, the Chinese attempted to change the way he thought.

Mr Ford was forced to spend nine hours a day examining his 'wrong' thinking. For part of that time, prisoners worked in small groups that would have to study specific subjects, such as the co-operative movement or the transition to socialism. The team would discuss an issue then come to a conclusion, which would then be shared with other groups who had been studying the same subject. There were also self-criticism sessions, where an individual would have to make a confession, however small. Prisoners had to reveal their innermost thoughts, which would be picked apart by fellow inmates, who would then suggest better ways of thinking. Even when everyone was locked up, cellmates would continue to question each other and debate. There was no escape. At first, Mr Ford seemed to believe that he could merely repeat the words he had to say to make it look as though he'd reformed, but he soon realised that this was not good enough; the guards were too clever. To compound the difficulty, prisoners did not simply have to parrot what they were told. They had to apply their new knowledge to their own situations and work out where they were going wrong.

It slowly dawned on the British man that he would have to genuinely believe what he was being told if he was to convince his captors that he really had changed his thinking and in the end, to his surprise, that's what started to happen. By Mr Ford's own admission, the communists had a well-thought-out worldview and he had little knowledge to contradict what they were saying. Marxism-Leninism appeared to have the answer to everything and so, little by little, he started to look at the world from a fresh perspective. At group meetings, he would feel a wave of emotion wash over him as the group chanted the slogans of a new world order. Later in life, Mr Ford said that he'd never been completely re-educated, that he always retained something of his old self, and following his release in 1955 he slowly reverted to the person he'd been before. But when I spoke to him, at the end of his long life and nearly 60 years after his internment by the Chinese, he still seemed a little embarrassed about how he'd nearly been turned into someone quite different.

The re-education system no longer exists in China as it did for Robert Ford; it was abolished in 2013. But that doesn't mean China's leaders have abandoned propaganda. Nothing could be further from the truth. It has merely adapted to a new age. China has an army of internet censors whose job is to weed out material that might corrupt the population. Often this job is done by internet companies themselves, whose in-house censors try to guess what might or might not be allowed, and sometimes cut more vigorously than any state censor. There are also thousands of people paid by the government to direct public opinion on social networking sites towards attitudes more favourable to the communist authorities. Rather than block a conversation, incurring the anger and suspicion of people having it, the party has realised that it's better to steer it in the desired direction. It wants people to think they are expressing their own opinions.

China's communists have always believed that educating people to think a particular way is an important tool to control society. They think it's as good as introducing laws to stop people doing something bad. In this respect, they're building on an ancient Confucian tradition, in which people were brought up to do the right thing because it was the right thing to do and not because you might get punished. In the West, we assume people have the propensity for behaving badly and so have laws to protect society. Of course, there are laws in China too, but there's also a deeply ingrained belief that people can be taught to be good. That's why propaganda is still so important.

Not Really Under Detention

Of course, propaganda doesn't always work. Sometimes people just can't be persuaded, however hard you try. So, while most citizens usually fall into line with what the government is thinking, there are occasions when they decide to challenge the authorities. In these situations, China's leaders have other tools they can employ to keep people in check; tools that reveal a darker side to their rule. These extra methods ultimately rely on force, finely calibrated for each situation and gradually increased if the circumstances demand. Very few Chinese people appear to realise that their leaders have these options at their fingertips and you can understand why. As a percentage of the whole population, hardly anyone is tortured or even mistreated and so, statistically, it's unlikely that any individual knows someone who has undergone such an ordeal. The Chinese government is understandably shy about its achievements in this field; it publishes no handy guidebook that details its many methods of control. But ultimately the communist party guarantees its rule by drawing upon the services of a sophisticated security machine, whose existence is there for anyone who cares to look.

The teacher is one of the few Chinese people I've met who is under no illusions about how the party maintains its grip on power and we would often talk about dissidents who'd disappeared or were facing lengthy prison sentences. He knew because he'd seen too much of the Chinese state not to know. He also knew because a friend had once worked at a school near one of China's strangest government departments: the State Bureau for Letters and Visits. Its name is misleadingly quaint. It sounds like a place where people might drop in for tea and meet long-lost friends but, in reality, it's the end of the road for desperate people who have reached the end of their tether.

This government department deals with the personal problems of people who have not been able to satisfactorily sort them out elsewhere. They are known as petitioners. From across China, they send their grievances by post or deliver them in person, in the hope that national leaders will give them some form of redress. Most end up disappointed. This is where the pensioners I'd heard about from Double River Farm in Heilongjiang were heading before they were kidnapped by local officials and taken home. They never even got to Beijing to register their complaints.

The teacher wanted to take me to the State Bureau for Letters and Visits so I could see it for myself. It's a depressing sight; hundreds of people wandering around wearing scruffy clothes and an air of being misunderstood. Most clutched dog-eared papers that in many instances document grievances dating back decades. During my time in China I met many petitioners and most seemed to believe that their cases had not been resolved simply because they hadn't managed to speak to the right official. They continue to travel to Beijing in the mistaken belief that national leaders will undo the errors of local officials when they finally get to see the evidence. They do not seem to realise that to maintain control the party often has to squash people with grievances, regardless of whether they have right on their side. That's why many petitioners appear confused when they are hassled and harried by the police for simply trying to bring their cases to the attention of those in charge.

As we drove slowly through the crowds, the teacher pointed out a plainclothes police officer. He spotted him easily because several years before he'd nearly been taken away by people doing a similar job. It had happened one day while he was waiting for the friend who worked at the nearby school to finish. As the teacher was standing around, someone approached him and asked him where he lived. He was dressed as a man and, as was often the case when he was in male clothing, he was looking a bit shabby. When he wore women's clothes he always looked the best he could, but as a man he sometimes gave the impression that basic hygiene was too much of a chore to bother with.

On that day, the teacher had obviously been mistaken for a petitioner. The matter could no doubt have been cleared up straight away, but at the time the teacher didn't fully realise the seriousness of his situation, so when asked where he lived he decided to give a cheeky response. He said he lived 'at home'. The teacher had only a little time to revel in his clever answer before a group of men lifted him up and tried to push him inside the back of a van. At this point, the teacher realised his mistake and shouted that he was from Beijing. He quickly reached into his pocket and pulled out his identity card, which proved he was telling the truth. The men put him down and he was allowed to go, but the experience brought it home to him that China's security machine is ever vigilant, particularly in sensitive places.

At the very lowest level, this machine gets its point across by merely suggesting that force can be used if required. Most people can be persuaded to adjust their behaviour by being reminded that there are consequences to their actions. The teacher learned that lesson outside the letters and visits office. The suggestion of force was also on show following the publication of Charter '08, a manifesto calling for political change in China. It was partly drafted by the activist Liu Xiaobo, who was detained on the eve of its publication and, as I've mentioned previously, was eventually sentenced to 11 years in prison, a punishment that earned him the Nobel Peace Prize. Liu Xiaobo became the movement's figurehead and was treated accordingly. To show they were still in control, the authorities must have felt they had no choice but to imprison him. The document though was also signed by several hundred other people in China, mostly academics, lawyers and activists. What should China's leaders do with them? They decided to tread softly and exert only gentle pressure. They wanted to get their point across without causing too much fuss.

In some cases the pressure was extremely gentle. One academic at the prestigious Chinese Academy of Social Sciences was told by his boss that he'd broken the law by signing. The boss also told him that he would no longer be allowed to write the foreword of a colleague's book; the right to publish had been withdrawn from everyone who had put their name to Charter '08. For academics who use the written word to spread their ideas this is a serious restriction. Another signatory, a lawyer, was asked to meet a security officer at a coffee shop for a chat. 'He didn't really say anything. He just listened to my reasons for signing and then left,' said the lawyer. A journalist who signed was not even required to meet anyone. He just knew that someone had turned up at his workplace asking for him. What must these citizens have thought in the days afterwards? What conversations did they have with their families? There was no violence, not even the threat of violence, but to know someone is watching you and taking a keen interest in your activities is an uncomfortable thought. For many signatories that was probably enough to warn them off from further activism.

I myself experienced this softly, softly approach. One morning as I was getting ready for work, I received a call from a foreign ministry official. A pleasant-sounding young woman asked in perfect English if I could meet her that afternoon in the Starbucks coffee shop near the ministry building. I agreed. Looking back, I suppose I had no choice, but it didn't feel like that at the time. Back then it felt like I'd simply received a call from an old friend who'd suggested we catch up. When we met, the official's manner and appearance only reinforced this perception. She was a good-looking woman in her thirties with an expensive haircut and well-chosen clothes. A silk scarf hung around her neck and she spoke quietly and thoughtfully. If there's such a thing as the opposite of an interrogation, then this was it. When we sat down she explained why she wanted to talk. In the weeks before there had been a lot of interest in the whereabouts of Gao Zhisheng, the detained lawyer I mentioned in Chapter Three. Many journalists had been asking questions about him at foreign ministry press briefings. I was among those who'd wanted to know where he was. The official's message delivered to me in Starbucks was simple: could I stop asking the foreign ministry about Mr Gao. She said no one there knew where the lawyer was so it was pointless to keep bringing him up.

I argued my case with the official, but when we parted it was on good terms. Despite the seriousness of our conversation, I didn't feel like I'd been threatened. It had all seemed so civilised. I stepped out onto the street and looked at a world that seemed to be going on as usual around me; shoppers drifted in and out of the department store next door, and car drivers honked their horns as they edged their way through Beijing's crowded streets. All of them were involved in their own lives; none of them knew about the conversation I had just had. Later, I realised that the location of our talk had led me to underestimate the meaning of what had happened. I'd simply not expected to come into contact with China's security machine in Starbucks. I blame George Orwell because his description of a totalitarian regime in *Nineteen Eighty-Four* had muddled my thinking. My subconscious self had assumed that secret operatives always work in dark corners, away from view. I expected them to announce who they were by their clothes, by the tone of their voice and by the threat of violence they carry around with them. The world in which they operate was supposed to be grim and full of proles, not peopled by happy shoppers wearing designer clothes. I had simply not imagined that a warning could come from a good-looking English-speaking woman in expensive clothes who ordered cappuccinos.

As a foreign journalist I could ignore the warning, safe in the knowledge that I wouldn't face the same punishment as a Chinese citizen in the same situation, but for those without the luxury of a foreign passport, the Starbucks chat would have taken on an entirely different and far more sinister meaning. I knew for a fact that Chinese activists, lawyers and those who worked for Western reporters were sometimes called in. These talks would usually take place at a public venue, such as a coffee shop or tea house, and usually everything would be conducted with the utmost politeness. The security services often tried to give the impression that they were just catching up on the latest gossip. It was informal and nothing serious. These meetings became known humorously as 'invitations for tea', but they were no laughing matter. The secret police would let their interviewees know that they knew many things about their private lives; where they lived, who their friends were and what their parents did. They would sometimes ask their targets to sign documents that required them to keep the get-together a secret. Understandably, these 'invitations for tea' create uncertainty, insecurity and fear in many of those who are questioned. It's a brave person who can simply brush aside such incidents and carry on as if nothing has happened.

A sad postscript to the story of the lawyer Gao Zhisheng, who the foreign ministry didn't want me to ask questions about, concerns his elder brother, a poor farmer from one of China's least-developed inland provinces, Shanxi. Unlike his educated sibling, Gao Zhiyi had little learning and seemed to know hardly anything outside the narrow confines of his own life. He was though a brave and determined man who had promised his mother just before she'd died that he would look after his younger brother, and that pledge meant something to him. I met him in Beijing one autumn. He'd travelled by long-distance bus to the capital to try to find his brother, and had spent several frustrating days visiting various police stations in the hope of getting some information. At one, officers had refused to hear his complaints and at another they'd told him that his brother had been lost, whatever that meant. At a third they had told the farmer to wait two months, but Gao Zhiyi had hardly any money, so after just a few days in Beijing he was forced to return home, having learned very little about his brother's fate.

When I met him he was just about to board his bus home. He looked understandably sad. 'I worry about him a lot. It's very painful not to know,' he said. He wondered why the police could not simply say what crime his brother had committed and put him on trial. He couldn't understand why no one could tell him what had happened. Like many Chinese people, he could see how powerful the security services are only when he had his own brush with them. In the end, Gao Zhiyi did find out where his brother was: the authorities eventually announced that they had imprisoned him. But that knowledge did not free either of the brothers from pain. After Gao Zhisheng was released, he was kept under house arrest in the faraway western region of Xinjiang. People knew where he was, but he was still under detention and out of reach.

As I've said, for most people who decide to heed that first encounter with the Chinese security services, that's often the end of the matter. They fall into line and their lives go on as before, but some people decide to ignore the warnings and so the machine applies a little more pressure. That might include nothing more than surveillance, but sometimes events are so serious that the authorities show a little more of what they are capable. That happened when suddenly and unexpectedly Tibetan monks and nuns began setting themselves alight in terrible personal protests against Chinese rule in the western part of Sichuan province. Most of these self-immolations happened in a mountainous region that's traditionally been considered part of Tibet. My colleagues and I decided to travel to the area to try to find out what was going on. We knew it wouldn't be easy. When a whole region proves troublesome, the Chinese authorities usually isolate it from the outside world. The security forces control who goes in and out, so as we drove towards the area we were aware that we might be stopped and sent back at any moment.

Our fears were soon realised. As we turned off the main highway and onto the road that led into the mountains I looked ahead and saw armed police officers stopping vehicles to check belongings and identity papers. We were three white faces in Western China (we'd left our Chinese colleagues at home for their own safety) and were picked out immediately. An armed man took our passports and told us to wait by our car. It wasn't long before we realised that for that day at least we were going no further. The police were taking our arrival seriously, something that became clear when a steady stream of expensive cars carrying local officials began to arrive at the checkpoint. Their smart occupants, who appeared annoyed at being called to a cold roadside, looked us up and down before disappearing into the police station next to the checkpoint. Eventually, our vehicle was escorted back to the nearby city of Ya'an so we could be questioned.

Chinese interrogations can sometimes take on a bizarre quality and when Mr Ma introduced himself we realised we were in the hands of someone who was not in complete control of his emotions. We were asked to sit at a table in a large open-plan office in a building that belonged to the public security bureau, China's police. We were separated from others in the office by a screen. Mr Ma put a video camera on top of an upturned bucket, turned it on and began the interview. He said we had broken Chinese law by not carrying with us a document called a Temporary Residence Certificate, a piece of paper that foreigners are required to have to prove where they live. I had the document, but it was at home in Beijing. This was the first time anyone had told me that we needed to carry it with us, so we asked Mr Ma to show us the relevant regulation that we had broken. He disappeared behind the screen before returning with a large law book. 'There,' he said, pointing halfway down an open page. I looked at the article in question and saw that it said people suspected of committing a crime had to have the document with them. 'But we're not suspects,' I said. We were merely driving down a public road, so why did we need the certificate? Mr Ma looked annoyed and again disappeared behind the screen.

The conversation with our interrogator carried on like this for nine hours. He would appear and make an accusation, or bring a new piece of information to support his case. We would respond, forcing him to go away again. Sometimes he was polite: 'Please, please, let's settle this like gentlemen,' he would say in his overwrought manner. Sometimes though he became angry, and would occasionally pick up the video recorder and shout straight into the lens. At one point, he disappeared for a while so I decided to go and look for him. On the other side of the screen I saw Mr Ma and his colleagues tucking into a takeaway dinner. Food is one of the main joys of life in China and I'd noticed before that there wasn't much, not even an interrogation, that could disrupt mealtimes. I asked Mr Ma if we could also have something to eat. 'You don't like Chinese food,' he shouted back, before relenting.

There were other lulls in the interrogation. During one we fell into conversation with another police officer who was helping his friend fill in a passport application in an adjacent office. The friend was going on holiday to India. My BBC colleague had previously been based in India and started telling the friend about the best places to visit. It was a long conversation that included the examination of railway timetables on the internet; the friend was keen to know whether it was possible to make several long journeys during his short time in India. I can remember thinking, not for the first time, that this wasn't how I imagined an interrogation should progress. We were relatively free to roam around the room and talk to other people and Mr Ma kept insisting that we were not really under detention, but he made it clear we couldn't leave either.

Eventually, in the early hours of the morning we were released. There was still time though for one more change of character from Mr Ma. He'd seen my colleague on television and wondered if it was possible to have a photograph with him. It was taken in front of a wall with a sign on it that showed we were in an office of the Chinese public security bureau. Mr Ma put his arm around my colleague's shoulder and smiled, as if posing with a great friend who he was not expecting to see again for some time. 'One more for luck,' he said after the first snap was taken. We left to warm hand-shakes. The Chinese driver we'd hired to take us to western

Sichuan was less pleased when we finally got back to the car. He'd also been detained and grumbled under his breath as we walked towards him. We asked him to collect us again the next morning and he agreed but, not unexpectedly, he didn't turn up.

Another problem with George Orwell's *Nineteen Eighty-Four* is that it gives the impression that the authoritarian state is omnipotent and always well organised. It knows everything, even your worst fear. China's state security machine is undoubtedly well funded and keeps close tabs on thousands of people, but there is occasionally room for mistakes. Sometimes its operatives seem as though they've served time with the Keystone Cops, the incompetent troop of police officers who starred in a series of silent Hollywood films at the beginning of the twentieth century. Over the following days, we would get many opportunities to see them in action.

We went back to Chengdu, the capital of Sichuan, to plan our next move and try to talk to some of the Tibetans who'd made their home in the city. It was clear from the beginning that we were being followed. The first inkling came from the driver of a taxi we'd hired to take us to the Tibetan quarter. As we were about to pay and get out, he took a call on his mobile phone. For a few moments he looked confused, as if the person on the other end of the line was someone he'd not expected to hear from. 'They're just getting out now,' he said. The police, or someone, was following us. We got out and walked quickly, making sharp turns down numerous side streets. We then got into another taxi and told the driver to make a series of random turns. We got out and walked through the front door of a hotel and out through the back, before getting into another taxi. Finally, when we thought we had shaken our tail, we dipped into a coffee shop to plan our next move.

Coffee shops are usually quite expensive places to eat and drink in China so customers tend to be well off. That's why a few minutes later my eyes were drawn to a young man in a large overcoat who appeared uncomfortable as he stood in the queue waiting to be served. He looked as though he was terrified someone would ask him what he wanted, and he was trying very hard not to look at us. Then we noticed a revealing word stitched in large letters on the inside of his coat. It said 'police' in English. So we hadn't managed to get rid of them after all. Later, as we were about to board a flight to another Tibetan area we saw the same man in the departure lounge.

We flew to a wild and rugged area called Jiuzhaigou because it was one of the few Tibetan areas of Sichuan that was open to foreigners. That's probably because it has become one of China's top tourist attractions. Jiuzhaigou's waterfalls, mountains and forests attract millions of visitors every year, even in winter when we were travelling. We checked into the Sheraton Hotel in the mistaken belief that five-star luxury might shield us a little from the police. It was late when we arrived and we were keen to hire a taxi for the next day. Fortunately, a friendly driver happened to be hanging around the hotel lobby so we booked him and asked him to come back early the following morning. The next day he was right on time, but as I was walking outside to greet him someone got into the passenger seat and the taxi sped off. I initially thought the driver had dropped us for a better fare, but a few minutes later he reappeared, looking less keen on the day's work ahead than he'd done the previous evening.

It soon became clear that somebody had spoken to our driver about us. He seemed increasingly agitated and kept coming up with ever more elaborate reasons why he couldn't drive us around that day. At one point he even said he had to go to a neighbouring province to deal with a family crisis. He was obviously scared and while listening to him tell us why he had to drop us by the side of the road, I found out why. I happened to glance down and saw a black wallet wedged between my seat and the taxi door. I surreptitiously fished it out and took a quick look. There was nothing inside except a police identity card, and I could see from the photograph that it belonged to the man who'd got in beside our driver earlier that morning. He worked at the Jiuzhaigou public security bureau. I quickly put the card in my pocket and wondered if the officer had realised he'd dropped his badge. I imagined him checking his pockets over and over again, and then in his mind retracing his steps. He must have shown the card to our driver and then dropped it as he tried to put it back into his pocket.

Shortly after I found the identity card the driver finally carried out his threat and dropped us by the side of the road. He telephoned his friend to ask him to come and pick us up and take us back to our hotel. He then drove off at speed. The natural hospitality foreigners usually find in Chinese people had been temporarily put aside by our driver because of the well-grounded fear that he might get into trouble. It seemed clear he wasn't telling the truth when he said he had a family problem to resolve in a nearby province, but it was pointless challenging him or making him lose face. We had just enough time to interview a few Tibetan villagers before the security services, pretending to be concerned local people, caught up with us and forced us back to the Sheraton. We had managed to do some filming for a television report, including shots of our pursuers, but we realised that getting this material back to the safety of Beijing would not be easy. Chinese police officers regularly force journalists to hand over their recording devices so they can delete any incriminating footage. So my colleague quickly took out the camera's memory card and hid it among his equipment. If we could get back to our room we could send it over the internet straight away, but would we be allowed to get there?

A handful of police officers were waiting for us when we returned. They blocked our path as we pushed our luggage trolley, the kind found only in expensive hotels, through reception. We all stood in the middle of the lobby, the police on one side of the trolley, us on the other. As we tried to push our luggage forward, they resisted. No one said anything and neither side used all their might to repel the other. It was as if we were all too polite to try too hard. Both sides gently pushed the trolley backwards and forwards for some time, as more and more hotel guests stopped to watch this strange stand-off. Perhaps out of embarrassment, the police finally gave in and let us through and from our room we sent our material to Beijing.

We returned to the lobby a little later to find a delegation of local government officials waiting for us. They'd turned up to find out what all the fuss was about and invited us to eat lunch with them in the expensive hotel dining room. It didn't seem like an invitation we could refuse and, anyway, by this time we were hungry. The tension of the earlier part of the day was now gone, and we sat and discussed Chinese affairs as though we were all disinterested observers; old friends enjoying the luxury of a good meal and time to talk. While we were eating, I received a call from the taxi driver who had earlier sped off to attend to that urgent family matter. He told me that he thought a friend had dropped his identity card in his car, but he couldn't find it. Did we know anything about it? He didn't mention that the 'friend' was a police officer. I wasn't about to admit that I was in possession of a police badge because someone could then accuse me of stealing it, so I said no. Later, on our way back to the airport in another taxi, we pushed the wallet under our driver's seat. It seemed the safest thing to do.

The incident with the pushing and shoving of the trolley brought to mind another bizarre encounter I'd had with China's security forces a few years earlier. I'd gone to interview a young, female activist called Zeng Jinyan, whose husband, also a campaigner, had been taken away by the authorities a few days earlier. The husband, Hu Jia, had been sitting at a computer in the dining room of the couple's small flat when officers barged in. At the time, his wife was in the bedroom feeding their two-and-a-half-month-old daughter. The couple were well known dissidents who'd originally been involved in promoting awareness about HIV/Aids, but had branched out into other areas of activism. Hu Jia began to document the sometimes small acts of disobedience that take place every day throughout China. His wife became just as prominent for blogging about their lives.

Before Hu Jia's arrest, the activists had spent many months under police surveillance. I once stood on the couple's balcony as Zeng Jinyan pointed out the plainclothes officers outside who monitored their every move. In an act of defiance, they'd managed to turn the tables on their watchers by secretly filming their movements. Hu Jia and his wife used this material to make a short documentary about their house arrest. They lived in a compound that was called, without any sense of irony, Freedom City, and so they entitled their film, *Prisoners of Freedom City*. It showed the extensive police operation that had been launched to keep watch on two campaigners who were relatively minor actors on China's political stage. Embarrassingly for the undercover police, the video did not detail their diligence at work. It showed them tucking into meals, playing cards and sleeping on the job.

When I went to see Zeng Jinyan about her husband's disappearance, the security net around her had tightened. It had once been possible to walk right up to her flat and ring the doorbell, but the police were by then stopping visitors getting to her apartment block. Telephone lines and internet access to her home had been cut. Eventually, the police would even prevent people from entering Freedom City, but that came later; I simply walked into the compound. Despite that, I wasn't sure if I'd be able to see Zeng Jinyan, but it turned out that I was lucky with my timing. The police had just allowed the activist to take her daughter down to the small garden in front of her block of flats, and as I approached I could see her walking around with the baby in her arms. A high fence made of steel bars stood between us, but as I got nearer I called out Zeng Jinyan's name and she turned around.

She walked towards me and we began chatting through the fence. She said she knew nothing about where her husband had been taken because her contact with the outside world had been severed, and the police weren't telling her anything. There was little time to say much more because four security operatives had by then noticed my arrival. They didn't want their charge talking to anyone, least of all a Western journalist. Something then happened that was similar in its strangeness to the incident with the trolley in the hotel in Jiuzhaigou. The policemen wanted to stop us talking and were prepared to use force, but they seemed timid about applying too much pressure. They came and stood between us, facing Zeng Jinyan and her baby and with their backs to me and the fence. They then started moving forwards very slowly, trying to force the activist back towards the entrance to her block of flats and away from me. They didn't touch her or say anything; they simply shuffled their feet, inch by inch, forming a human wall that ever-so-gradually pushed Zeng Jinyan in the desired direction. The tiny activist had no alternative but to keep stepping backwards.

As this went on, the distance between us kept growing. The campaigner tried to shout through gaps between the four police officers, but they'd linked arms to form a compact unit. Had they practised this manoeuvre before? 'I try to be strong because I need to feed my baby,' the young woman managed to shout out. She was obviously distressed and there seemed much she wanted to tell me, but her guards kept pushing her slowly back and eventually I couldn't make out what she was trying to say. Finally, she disappeared into her apartment block and out of sight. It was a curious encounter, not least because of the way in which the police had dealt with the incident. Obviously, they'd wanted the activist to do as she was told without having to manhandle her in front of a witness, but I couldn't help thinking the episode revealed something more profound beyond that practical consideration.

To me, the incident laid bare the government's claim to be a force for good. It was proof that it had lost its moral authority. Chinese people often emphasise the civilised and civilising aspects of their national identity; their gentleness and their pacifism. China's rise, we are constantly reminded, is a peaceful rise. No one has anything to fear. If that's true, why was it necessary to treat a young woman and her baby so badly? Neither had been charged with any offence. The actions of the four undercover policemen also seemed to suggest that they knew they were doing something wrong. If Zeng Jinyan really had been an enemy of the people, they could have just picked her up and carried her away with a clear conscience. There would have been no need to shuffle her out of sight.

It's not only Chinese security agents who can act in strange and silly ways. Journalists are capable of that too. I look back with embarrassment on one particular incident when my colleagues and I travelled to Shandong province to try to interview a blind activist lawyer called Chen Guangcheng. By the time I tried to talk to him, Mr Chen had become something of a cause célèbre, whose fame extended far beyond China's borders. He had taught himself the law and made a name for himself by representing women who'd accused the authorities of forcing them to undergo abortions or sterilisation procedures. These cases revealed one of the murkier sides of China's strict family planning policies: the sometimes brutal and cruel methods undertaken by officials to make sure no family had more children than was allowed. For his trouble, Mr Chen had been sent to prison, for the spurious charges of disrupting traffic and damaging property. After his release he became a prisoner in his own home, watched day and night by dozens of security personnel. The world was alerted to his plight by a video, smuggled out of his village, showing plainclothes officers peeping through the windows into the house he shared with his wife and daughter.

It was at this point that Chen Guangcheng's story began to resemble a film script. Despite being blind, he planned and executed a daring escape. After lying in bed for several days pretending to be ill, he fled his prison home by jumping over a wall and into a pigsty. He lay in hiding all day and then, under the cover of darkness, left the village. His guards had not missed him during the day because they had mistakenly thought he was still sick in bed. How a blind man managed to evade such tight security remains a mystery and, no doubt, an embarrassment to the Chinese authorities. With the help of friends, Mr Chen made his way to Beijing, where he sought sanctuary in the US embassy. He had chosen a good time to escape. He was ushered into the American compound just as the US Secretary of State at the time, Hillary Clinton, was about to arrive in the Chinese capital for an official visit. Mr Chen's presence at the embassy caused a major diplomatic incident. After a few days he decided to leave his refuge, but when the Chinese kept him incommunicado in the hospital where he'd been sent for treatment, he decided he would rather leave the country altogether. He flew to America with his family a few weeks later.

I had gone to speak to Mr Chen before his dramatic escape. My colleagues and I tried to visit him while he was still under house arrest. We knew that others had made the same journey and had been turned away, sometimes violently, so we weren't expecting to get close enough to the lawyer to actually speak to him. But we thought we had to try anyway. To record our journey into Mr Chen's village, we'd put cameras around our car, to capture any assault that might come from the authorities. As we drove on towards our destination I prematurely congratulated myself on our cleverness, while bracing myself for what might lie ahead.

There are few reliable maps in China so we didn't know the exact location of Mr Chen's house but, as we drove into his village, a solution presented itself in the shape of a group of men who just happened to be lounging around at the side of the road. Our driver, who we'd brought from Beijing, suggested we stop and ask them which way to go. It was only when I watched the driver's familiar gait as he ambled up to the group that it crossed my mind that this might not be a good idea. Who were these people standing doing nothing by the side of the road? Why did they have a menacing air? Were we about to ask directions from the wrong people?

We had to wait only a few seconds to find out. As soon as the men looked towards our car they realised who we were and rushed towards us. We briefly thought about locking the doors, but quickly decided that it would be futile, and possibly dangerous, to resist. They ordered us out of the car in language that didn't encourage argument and then searched the inside, putting our cameras and other equipment into a large sack. They refused to say who they were or on whose authority they were acting, and they carried nothing to identify themselves; they wore T-shirts and jeans, not uniforms, but it was clear they were acting on someone's orders.

They had sprung into what appeared to be well-planned action when our driver approached them. One man had a walkie-talkie and used it to speak to someone else, somewhere else, when they found out we were journalists. They refused to answer our questions, leaving us standing by the side of the road waiting for the next move. Surprisingly, a few minutes later they handed back all our equipment, including the cameras that had caught their assault. They hadn't bothered to delete the material. They told us to leave the village and we didn't argue; we simply jumped into our car and did as we were told. We knew we already had proof that these people existed. We could show that the Chinese state had employed thugs to keep the world away from the blind lawyer, a man Chinese officials in Beijing were insisting was a free man.

Our trip had been a salutary reminder that even the best-thought-out plans can be derailed by a little stupidity. Why on earth had we not thought about how we'd get to Mr Chen's house once we'd arrived in his village? It was also a reminder that violence is something the Chinese state is prepared to engage in if the situation requires, and officials are more than willing to act outside the law if they feel there's a need. The people who stopped us did not identify themselves as police officers and did not attempt to mask their actions under the cloak of legality; they were thugs standing by the side of the road threatening anyone who might try to speak to Chen Guangcheng. A few months later back in Beijing a foreign ministry official tried to argue that the men we'd encountered were local people who had acted on their own initiative after becoming angry at the number of outsiders arriving to see the blind lawyer. He and I both knew that was rubbish.

What did all the violence and nastiness mean? Chinese

people are generally peaceful and most seem to think the current government is genuinely trying to improve their lives. If there was a general election tomorrow, the Chinese Communist Party would have a good chance of winning. Why then does the party feel it has to watch, harass and imprison people who most of the time are merely asking for a little fairness? I remember being surprised when Zeng Jinyan, the activist with the baby, told me that she didn't want to overthrow the system, she just wanted to tweak it. With a little more thought, the party could co-opt all those activists, lawyers and campaigners instead of turning them into enemies. The fact that it doesn't seems to be down to pure paranoia. China's current leaders want to stay in power and they are prepared to crush even the tiniest challenge to their authority, whether real or imagined. Whatever anyone says, Chinese citizens are just a few poorly chosen words or an unwise action away from detention.

A Business Opportunity

The teacher's story had turned quite dark. His anecdotes about his time at the propaganda department and his brush with detention at the petitioners' office had led me into unpleasant and occasionally sickening corners of Chinese society. These are shadowy places inhabited by secret police operatives and citizens who've somehow failed to benefit from China's boom time. I often wondered whether the retelling of these people's stories, which I did regularly in my job as a correspondent, had given me a twisted view of China because there was another far brighter side to life: one of optimism and hope and improving standards of living.

For every person who's been arrested or hassled by the authorities, there are hundreds, perhaps thousands, of others who are more or less happy with how their country and their lives are progressing. China's political system has changed little since 1949; the communist party retains as firm a grip as ever on the levers of power, but economic reforms have changed the country beyond recognition, and mostly for the better. The credit for this must go to the group of elderly leaders, led by Deng Xiaoping, who took power after Mao died in 1976. They gradually dismantled Chairman Mao's Cultural Revolution, imprisoned his most ardent followers and initiated a transformation that Mao would surely have fought to prevent. Praise must also go to China's weary population, who embraced change with enthusiasm after years of deprivation and political chaos.

When the reforms came, they had the determination and resourcefulness to take advantage of them. They sometimes even initiated change themselves. The story that encapsulates this doggedness more than any other is the tale of Xiaogang, a tiny village in Anhui province. It's a story that's well known in China and often used by the authorities to show how the government has adapted to changing circumstances. It's worth retelling because it really does capture the resolve shown by Chinese people at the time.

Xiaogang was poor in a way that was once normal in China, but is now difficult to imagine. In the famine that swept the country between 1958 and the early 1960s, the result of Mao's decision to force everyone into communes, 67 of the village's 120 people died of starvation. Even when the famine was over, times were never good. Land was owned by the commune and people earned points by working in its fields. These points could be exchanged for food, but there was hardly ever enough to go around. Sometimes the harvest was so bad that villagers had to roam the countryside begging for food. Families would boil leaves and eat them with salt, or grind down roasted bark and use it as flour. Even by the late 1970s the situation was little better, so the people of Xiaogang decided to take action. In December 1978, out of sheer desperation, they signed a contract – those who couldn't write used thumbprints – agreeing to divide the commune's land into family plots. The villagers made a commitment to continue supplying the state with the quota of crops they'd already agreed to provide, but they would keep the rest for themselves.

At the time this was illegal, and the villagers knew they faced lengthy prison sentences and even the death penalty if the authorities decided to look unfavourably on their experiment. Neighbours promised to look after each other's children if the parents were taken away. The villagers' plan also contradicted the political thinking that had governed their lives for decades. Working for yourself was supposed to be part of the bad old system that Chairman Mao had tried to eradicate. Fortunately, local officials turned a blind eye to what was going on in Xiaogang, deciding to wait and see if the new system improved yields. It did. Spectacularly.

In 1979, the grain harvest was six times higher than it had been the previous year. The villagers had transformed their fortunes by changing only one thing: the way in which they were organised. Instead of working for the collective, everyone was now working, at least part of the time, for themselves. If they laboured hard and were lucky, their families would have more to eat and more to sell. The system soon spread to other parts of the country and by the early 1980s it had been endorsed by China's top leaders. Farmland in China today is still divided up into family plots. Hunger had led the villagers of Xiaogang to take a risk and dream up an agricultural revolution.

The can-do spirit shown in Xiaogang and other places infected the nation. After years of suppressing their individualistic instincts, people could now begin to express themselves in so many different ways. They believed they could do almost anything and, for a change, the government encouraged them. In the years after the reforms began, the old system started to break down one step at a time. Under Mao, farmers had lived in communes while 'work units' employed city people. Both organisations were more than simply places to work: they oversaw every aspect of a person's life. They provided people with housing, medical care, a canteen and perhaps even a nursery for their children. They would take workers on trips and make sure they broke no laws. Slowly though, these institutions started to disappear.

A Business Opportunity

The idea that individuals could choose their own place to live and work would once have found no favour in China, but as the old way of doing things gradually faded away people began to forge their own lives. They bought their own homes, started businesses and looked for more satisfying ways to spend their days. Like everyone else, the teacher was swept up in this euphoria. His university degree proved to be the key to success and fulfilment. He worked in the food company's propaganda department until the year 2000 when he left to become a full-time journalist on a magazine. A few years later he changed careers, becoming a teacher at one of Beijing's most prestigious universities. He taught Chinese to foreigners, supplementing his income with private students, which is how I had the good fortune to meet him. He wrote a book that explored the most commonly used phrases in Chinese. As he gained confidence in himself, the teacher also dreamed of becoming a businessman. He wanted to emulate the success of China's newly minted millionaires. With this though, he over-reached himself. It was a reminder that bright ideas don't always turn out well.

China's current economic success seems even more amazing when you realise that, through the ages, business people have been looked down upon. Grubbing around with money was never seen as an occupation to aspire to in ancient China. The teacher seemed to embody this point of view. He saw himself as something of a gentleman scholar and appeared to share the traditional disdain for business. The Chinese communists built on this contempt for private wealth and commerce. Put simply, they saw it as wrong. At various points during their rule, business people, financiers and sometimes even anyone with money could end up in prison – or worse. Many rural landowners were executed following the communists' victory in China's civil war in 1949. Deng Xiaoping began to change the traditional communist view of private business, but it was only in the late 1990s under President Jiang Zemin that the party realised it had to make peace with those who were driving economic growth. Mr Jiang decided to welcome them into the communist party. It was another ideological somersault, another example of 'socialism with Chinese characteristics'.

In some respects, President Jiang's decision was simply a reflection of what was going on across China. When Deng Xiaoping called for reform and opening up in the late 1970s many of China's citizens responded like ducks to water. Some, like the villagers of Xiaogang, even drove change themselves. Despite years of left-wing rhetoric, ordinary people became the pioneers of a new business-orientated China. The teacher admired these resourceful entrepreneurs and one day asked me to lunch at a very special Beijing restaurant, which billed itself as China's first privately owned eatery to open up after the Cultural Revolution. When we visited, the Yuebin restaurant was still being run by the couple who had opened it in 1980. At that time the idea of change was still new and so just getting the business off the ground had been no easy task. The couple were initially refused a licence to operate and some of their neighbours reacted angrily, seeing this private enterprise as a betrayal of communism. Eventually though, good cooking attracted paying customers and the restaurant's reputation grew.

Yuebin looked as though it hadn't changed in decades. It was furnished with simple wooden tables and chairs, which had been pushed together tightly so as many customers as possible could be crammed into the tiny dining area. The walls were whitewashed and there was a dirty curtain hanging in the doorway between the kitchen to the dining room. Bills were still tallied using an abacus, but the owners relied on modern technology to make sure no customer tried to spend a fake banknote; each one was checked in an electronic machine before the cashier would accept it. Trust is sometimes in short supply in China and these machines were everywhere. The restaurant was busy with people who wanted to sample food that was both cheap and delicious. Some diners had taken taxis from far away after hearing about Yuebin's history, others were regulars who lived just a few steps away.

As we tucked into some of our favourite dishes – spicy aubergine, winter melon and braised tofu – the teacher relaxed and started talking about what he'd been like as a child. He said he'd been quiet and didn't like to join group activities. If there was a class meeting he wouldn't speak up. The teacher said his mother had told him that he had the temperament of a girl. He might have been quiet when he was younger, but the teacher can now talk for his country – and he's nosy. As we ate, he kept looking round to see what other people were eating. Two men in suits who'd ordered a table full of dishes caught his eye. Chinese people regularly over-order in restaurants; they do it to show their wealth, and it was obvious that this pair were not going to finish their meal. He didn't know them, but the teacher, on this occasion dressed as a man, fired off a question. 'How many dishes have you got there?' he shouted across the room in a tone that implied they had too many. 'What's it to you?' one of them replied.

The restaurant might still be the same as it was in 1980, but China isn't, a change that was neatly put into words by Guo Peiji, the man who'd opened Yuebin with his wife all those years ago. Mr Guo said everyone's lives had now improved. 'Who now can't afford the prices at my restaurant?' he asked rhetorically. 'Today, even poor people are richer than the rich people of yesterday.' The teacher had seen that too. That's perhaps why he'd tried his own hand at acquiring wealth, even though he didn't have a real passion for making money.

I asked so many questions about his business venture that the teacher eventually promised to show me more. That's how I ended up on a depressing drive to the place where he'd tried and failed to become rich.

The countryside to the north of Beijing is mountainous and beautiful. The air is noticeably fresher than in the city and the views are staggering. Orchards cling to hillsides and it's not unusual to round a corner and see China's Great Wall snaking over the distant mountaintops. The landscape to the south of the capital, though, is flat and not nearly as interesting; endless fields of corn crisscrossed by motorways that connect Beijing with the rest of China. The villages to the north retain features of China's rural past; giant millstones that were once turned by donkeys still lay abandoned in the centre of many, but to the south the villages are bigger and more connected to the modern world. Workshops clutter the roadsides, their industry spilling out into the streets in front, and the land is pockmarked with development at various stages of completion.

On the day we drove south, the teacher had dressed up. He wore a see-through T-shirt and a knee-length black and white polka dot skirt. The white beads that hung around his neck added a touch of class, but his attire looked totally out of place in the colourless surroundings he drove us through. His style of driving – we seemed to lurch forward at speed only to slow unexpectedly – did nothing to add to the experience. 'Have you actually passed your driving test?' I asked the teacher. He just laughed. A thick blanket of smog hung over the countryside, completely obscuring the sun that was presumably up there somewhere. As usual, it made me feel miserable. Travel usually improves my mood, but not that day. As the teacher hummed a traditional Chinese tune, I sat silently by his side.

The idea behind the teacher's business was simple: to set

up a place in the countryside where city people could escape to at weekends. They would be able to eat local food and enjoy a gentler pace of life. Hundreds of families had already set up similar businesses in the mountains to the north of Beijing. These places were part restaurant, part hotel and part karaoke bar. They offered the farmers who opened them the chance to make the kind of money they could never hope to earn by tilling the fields. Their success rested on a growing realisation among many in China's emerging middle class: urban life offers modern conveniences, but comes at a price. People in the city have to endure crowded buses, polluted air and a depressing lack of green space. The Chinese have for centuries revelled in the joy of simply observing nature, but that's difficult to do if your apartment is 20 floors up and much of the time the smog is so bad you can't see the tower block next to you. So, those with enough money began to look for a weekend getaway, and the rural homestay business was born. The teacher had noticed the trend and decided to replicate this successful business model to the south of Beijing, in an area of Hebei province near his family's ancestral village.

I first heard about the business when it was all over. One day, the teacher arrived for our usual Chinese lesson clutching a piece of paper that had printed on it a list of items for sale: tables, chairs, a sofa and various other odds and ends. One item caught my eye: a karaoke machine. When I asked the teacher why he even had a karaoke machine to sell, he quickly abandoned that day's lesson plan and began telling me the story of his failed business, which had opened to great fanfare in late 2010. One of the teacher's relatives supplied the building and he provided 100,000 yuan (about £10,000) to transform it into a relaxing destination that people might enjoy at the end of a long working week. The teacher's homestay offered food and singing, and later on he intended to add rooms where people could stay for the night. The teacher's wife, who belonged to the shrewder half of the marriage, had advised caution. She told her husband to sign a contract with whoever he did business with, relative or not, but the teacher ignored the advice and paid for it later. Despite great hopes, the business did not last long; there were simply not enough customers. Less than a year after it opened up, the homestay closed down.

The teacher partly blamed the relative, who'd decided to rent the building to someone else when he saw just how little money they were making and how few customers they were attracting. With no contract to break, the relative had simply done what he wanted. 'I trusted him,' the teacher told me, realising his error far too late to be of any use. In the end, he lost most of his initial investment. When I saw him with his list, he was trying to calculate how much he could recoup by selling some of the more moveable fittings. When the selling was done, he managed to get back just 8,000 yuan (£800). Surprisingly, he didn't seem as disappointed as I would have expected. 'It just didn't work out,' was all he said, showing a stoicism and resignation that I'd seen him display on many previous occasions.

Despite the failure, the teacher was still happy for me to see his former business premises. That's why we were driving south into Hebei. The journey allowed me to see why people looking for a weekend break would rather head north. The teacher had simply chosen the wrong place to start his business. Those feelings were confirmed when our car pulled off the main road and into an area of land in front of several shabby single-storey buildings. 'That's it,' said the teacher, pointing to a badly constructed, windowless structure located right next to a rubbish dump. It didn't look like anywhere anyone would want to visit to shake off the dust of the city. We were just a few metres from the main road, on which lorries zoomed past every few seconds. The highway had been banked up and so stood taller than the surrounding countryside, giving anyone unfortunate enough to be nearby a wonderful view – and sound and smell – of the trucks as they trundled by.

I turned around to get a proper look at the building, but before I could say anything I noticed the business next door: a coffin maker. Several large caskets were stacked up outside, and the sound of a buzz saw suggested more were at that very moment being prepared. The craftsmanship looked good and I thought that perhaps when I go I wouldn't mind being buried in something as ornate as that, but then I remembered why I was there. 'Why did you open a business next to a coffin maker?' I asked the teacher. Many Chinese people are still very superstitious and try to avoid any connection with death or dying. Even modern buildings often lack a fourth floor because in Chinese the word for 'four' sounds like the word for 'death'. No one wants to live or work on the floor of death. So why would anyone want to open a restaurant next to a shop selling coffins? The teacher shrugged. 'It was the only building my relative had,' he offered, by way of explanation.

We didn't stay long; there was nothing much to see, apart from a failed dream in the shape of a badly-put-together building. I consider the teacher to be an intelligent man with a fair amount of common sense, but it was clear that when he'd invested his money in the homestay business those qualities had temporarily deserted him. Afterwards, he claimed he hadn't been that interested making money. He said he'd gone into the business for something to do; more a hobby than anything. I suspected he was not being entirely truthful. No one likes to lose so much money so quickly. As we drove away, the teacher told me that our trip was not yet done. He was keen to see the cook who'd once fed the visitors at his failed enterprise. She was still working nearby. His business had not been a success, but he'd made a friend and didn't want to go home without seeing her.

The cook was working for a company that employed half a dozen men to crush large stones into smaller pieces of rubble for the construction industry. Her job was to provide the workers with three meals a day, seven days a week. As we drove up to her new workplace, I saw that it perfectly encapsulated the spirit of desolation that had slowly settled over me during the journey from Beijing. The workers were toiling in a muddy field dotted with giant potholes. There was little vegetation and the few trees that had survived were coated in dirt. It reminded me of the unreal landscapes that live on in black and white photographs of First World War battlefields. The men were working next to a giant crushing machine, shovelling large stones onto a conveyor belt that dropped them into the business part of the machinery. The rocks were pounded into more manageable sizes and then spat onto another conveyor belt, which deposited them several metres away on top of an ever-increasing pile. Lorries bounced in and out of the site, splashing up water that had settled in the potholes. They loaded the stones and carried them away. For the men who toiled there, it was simple but back-breaking work.

The teacher and I found the woman who'd been charged with feeding the workers in a building that seemed to be in the process of falling down. It wasn't entirely clear what was holding it up. There was a huge crack in one wall and the doorframe was so wonky that the door didn't shut properly. The boss had clearly not considered it worthwhile buying any furniture; the inside was virtually bare. Dirt and rubbish provided the only decoration. Poverty in films often looks noble and clean, but here it was just wretched.

We found the cook in the kitchen, doing her best with

what little equipment had been placed at her disposal. There was no cooker to speak of, just a one-ring stove attached to a rubber tube that led to a large gas cylinder. She had a gigantic wooden chopping board and an impressive looking cleaver, but little else in the way of utensils. The cook herself was a large and nimble woman who smiled a lot. She was pleased to see her old friend and it was clear from their easy manner that they'd been close. She must have been familiar with the teacher's love of women's clothes because she made no comment about what he was wearing. They chatted as she worked. We'd arrived just before lunchtime and the cook was moving quickly between wok and chopping board. The men outside were working hard and would probably not want to wait for their food.

She wasn't preparing an extravagant meal: pancakes made of flour and a popular dish made up of thinly sliced potatoes and chillies. As she stir-fried the potatoes I noticed she sprinkled in a dash of monosodium glutamate. The teacher, perhaps remembering his previous job, smiled. When it was ready the workers filed in, took their rations quickly and without fuss, and then shuffled out to eat in their dormitory. I hadn't realised people slept in the building too. The food had been prepared in basic surroundings and made from cheap ingredients, but when I tasted some of the leftovers I discovered it was delicious. I was reminded again that the quality of a kitchen's food in China usually has little to do with the look of the kitchen itself.

With her work for the moment done, the cook asked the teacher and me to eat with her at a next-door restaurant, which served quite a bit more than the simple fare she'd just prepared for the workers. We ordered pig's trotters, grapes in syrup and the local tofu speciality. There were other dishes too; far more than we could eat. I asked the cook if the workers, who were by then back at work shovelling stones, ever ate like this. 'I have to keep to a budget, but sometimes we have meat,' she said, as she poured herself a glass of strong rice wine. Later, I found out it was the cook's birthday and I felt bad that I'd implied she ate better than the workmen. Times are still tough for China's poorest people and I couldn't blame her for enjoying a good meal, particularly as it was her birthday. I also told myself that Chinese people are generous to a fault when it comes to hospitality. The cook had been pleased to see the teacher and obviously wanted us all to dine well.

If she was annoyed by my comment about the food, to her credit she didn't show it. The cook was in a talkative mood and words poured out as quickly as the liquor from the rapidly emptying bottle on the table. Her story reminded me of so many others I'd heard in China. The booming economy offers everyone the hope of more money and a better life, but society has fractured in many unforeseen ways. The burden of these changes often falls heaviest on the poorest sections of society. Over the last three decades, hundreds of millions of rural people have left the land in search of new opportunities in richer urban areas. The high price they often pay for higher wages is a splintered family life. The cook said her husband worked on a construction site in Beijing. She rarely saw him, even though he only lived a couple of hours' drive away. She said her grown-up son lived in the capital, and like his father also worked on a construction site, but in a different part of the city. Three people, three separate locations. '*Mei banfa*,' I muttered to no one in particular.

Life can sometimes be sweet even in the most depressing of surroundings, and I began to notice that the cook didn't seem too concerned that her husband lived in Beijing. Consolation for her single-person's existence seemed to have presented itself in the shape of the middle-aged company foreman, who'd joined us for the birthday meal. He'd been hovering around the kitchen ever since we arrived, helping to prepare the men's food and occasionally exchanging furtive looks with the cook. As more rice wine was ordered and consumed, it became increasingly clear that the foreman and the cook enjoyed a special relationship. The glances between them became less secretive and they looked as though they were playing footsie under the table.

The liquor seemed to embolden the foreman, or perhaps it was his close proximity to the cook. Whatever it was, he stood up, swayed a little and then gave a short speech. 'You'll have to come again,' he told us. 'Don't worry about food and lodgings, I'll take care of it. My word around here counts.' He then exchanged another longing look with the cook. The first thing the teacher asked me when we'd left the restaurant was whether I'd noticed what was going on. I told him it would have been difficult not to. The teacher explained that when his homestay business had still been open, he'd had many conversations with the cook and she'd confided in him. She'd told him that her husband was too skinny to satisfy her voracious sexual appetite and the teacher suspected she was now having an affair with the foreman. I thought he was probably right. As we drove away, the cook and her companion stood close to each other as they waved us off.

I thought afterwards that the trip to the stone-pummelling yard ought to be on the itinerary of every visiting foreign dignitary who goes to China. People arrive constantly from abroad to see the Chinese economic miracle for themselves, no doubt hoping to return with knowledge that can be put to good use in their own countries. But these VIP visitors mostly stay in Beijing. They enjoy well-appointed hotels and good food, and usually meet their welcoming hosts in smart offices. They see the impressive results of Chinese labour, but don't often get to poke around in the places where most of the work is actually done. If they do travel outside the capital, it's usually on well-organised trips that leave out capitalism's grimier aspects. The cook's new place of employment offered the kind of insight that weeks of meetings might never reveal. I saw hard work and determination. There were new opportunities and the chance to make money. There was sacrifice, but also fun and occasionally good food. Sometimes there was dirt, lots of it. It was new China reflected in one of its shabbier workplaces.

This new way of life has not been welcomed by everyone. There are now more opportunities, but there are also more risks and increased pressure, and there are still some who hanker after the certainties of the recent past. I saw that when I visited the village of Nanjie in central China's Henan province for a TV report to mark a communist party anniversary. The village was proud to be one of the last remaining communes in the whole of the country. The idea behind these social units was simple. Everything was pooled, including farm equipment, animals, even pots and pans, just as they had been in the village of Xiaogang, just as they had been in Mao's home village. People didn't work for themselves; they worked for the commune. In return, the commune provided them with all they needed. Meals were served in communal halls and welfare benefits, such as education and healthcare, were supplied by the state.

When the communes were set up in the late 1950s they were supposed to usher in a socialist paradise, but as an economic policy they proved disastrous, as I've already explained. Predictably, people's dedication to their work was not all it should have been because they knew they would get fed whether they worked fast or slow. There was little incentive to show initiative. Communes were disbanded when Mao died and Deng Xiaoping took charge, but in a few places, including Nanjie, they've lingered on, employing the language and some of the policies of the old system.

A Business Opportunity

It was clear Nanjie was different from the moment my colleagues and I drove through its gates. Immediately before us stood a giant statue of Mao, with one arm outstretched as if welcoming weary travellers. The statue had been placed in a large square flanked by portraits of communist heroes. Karl Marx and Friedrich Engels were there, both wearing impressively bushy Victorian beards. The founders of the Soviet Union, Vladimir Lenin and Joseph Stalin, also looked on. Images of Mao and his fellow left-wing icons still dot the landscape in other places in China. They are reminders of a time when China's citizens still believed in a socialist future. For most people, those dreams are dead, but in Nanjie the world's communist heroes and the ideas they espoused still seemed to mean something.

The village grew crops, such as corn, and had a number of small factories producing a bewildering array of products. Hot sauce, rice wine and chocolate were just some of the items that came off the production lines. The villagers even made noodles that were exported to capitalist America, although no one could quite explain what Chairman Mao might have thought of that. The 4,000 or so people who lived in Nanjie worked in the fields or in the factories. In exchange, they received a small wage, but also an impressive range of welfare benefits. They paid no rent and nothing towards their bills. Their children studied in schools that charged no hidden fees (unlike schools elsewhere in China) and if anyone was sick the commune paid the bill. If life in the commune was limited and a little dull, it was still largely free from the worries that constantly nag people on the outside. Villagers said they would rather be in than out.

Nanjie was not quite the socialist utopia its inhabitants believed. There were rumours that the commune was in serious debt and only survived because it was being bank-rolled by the local government. It also traded on its unique status in a way that would have been impossible if all rural areas were still divided into communes. The village attracted thousands of tourists keen to see one of the last examples of a bygone era. To accommodate them, the commune had built a hotel, which was staffed by workers wearing green military-style uniforms; clothes that might have been worn half a century ago. Workers at the commune's supermarket wore similar outfits, no doubt adding to the experience of visitors who bought products wrapped in packages marked with Nanjie's distinctive logo. The village was clearly benefiting from the phenomenon known as 'red tourism', where visitors descend on the hundreds of venues and locations associated with China's communist heritage. The ideology that brought these places into existence has mostly been abandoned, but people remain curious about the past they've just discarded. These tourists were helping Nanjie survive.

To criticise Nanjie because it's not really communist would be to miss its significance. The village might not be a perfect example of communal living, but it illustrates a fear that lurks in the hearts of many Chinese people: that something worthwhile has been lost during the country's economic transformation. Few people would want to return to the chaotic times under Chairman Mao, but those same people might also yearn for certainty in some aspects of their lives. The constant battle to secure a good school for children or proper care for elderly parents is one that many people would rather not engage in. They'd prefer the state to sort it out. There are also those who desire something more than material wealth, a goal other than money. At least when China was still communist, the party appeared to be building something worthwhile. Life today has more possibilities, but it's also more uncertain and for some people it has far less meaning.

I knew exactly why the people of Nanjie enjoyed their

cosseted lives because I'd experienced something similar when my wife and I worked at the *China Daily* in Beijing. The newspaper is controlled by the government and run as an old-fashioned 'work unit', or *danwei* as they are known in Chinese. As I've said, at one time almost everyone in China belonged to either a *danwei* or a commune. It felt a little like living in an extended family, where the burdens of life would be shared, and mostly by the work unit. Ours had a canteen that served breakfast, lunch, dinner and supper. All a worker had to do was turn up with their own bowl. The food was delicious – and cheap. It was all subsidised. We also had a rent-free flat where all the bills were paid. If something went wrong I could pick up the phone and call a workman who'd pop along and fix whatever needed mending. There were gifts at Christmas and Chinese New Year, and day trips to interesting places. Ping pong tables allowed us to while away a lunch break and there was a garden to sit in. As foreigners we were given special treatment, but Chinese workers enjoyed similar benefits that extended into retirement.

Life in a work unit could sometimes be a little claustrophobic and there was a sinister side that was far less appealing than the benefits. Managers were involved in our lives in ways that would be unthinkable in the West, where a boss's control extends no further than the factory gates or the office door. We were expected to behave in an appropriate manner and told off if we didn't. It's worse for Chinese people. A *danwei* can control and influence parts of their lives that have nothing to do with work. Still, the benefits are potentially huge and many people still talk longingly of the 'iron rice bowl', the phrase that describes cradle-to-grave benefits offered by work units.

Just before I left China I went to the wedding of the daughter of an old friend. He was more than seventy at the time and slightly out of touch with the China of his daughter's generation. When he stood up and gave his speech he urged his son-in-law to find a suitable *danwei* that would take care of him and his new wife. There are a dwindling number of work units now and the couple would have found it difficult to find one, even if they'd wanted to be employed by such an intrusive institution, but my friend was merely expressing a desire that still exists in China – a need for security.

The teacher and I chatted about these issues as we drove away from his former cook and her presumed lover. He was as fascinated as I was about the changes taking place in China and how his own life had been shaped by this revolution. We were heading back to Beijing, but before we'd been going for more than a few minutes the teacher turned the car off the main road and drove down a narrow track flanked on either side by tall trees. I'd forgotten that he'd opened his homestay business near the village his family had once lived in for generations. That's where he was taking me.

His grandfather had left the village in the 1920s or 30s – the teacher couldn't remember which. He'd travelled to Beijing to take up a job as second in command at a rickshaw company. The rickshaw is still a symbol of imperial oppression in East Asia. The image that comes readily to mind is that of a barefooted coolie sweating as he pulls along a fat Westerner, who seems oblivious to the fate of the man doing all the work. I travelled to China as a student and remember having a bad-tempered argument with friends about whether it was right to take a bicycle rickshaw. Some of us, including me, argued that it was fine if we paid well, others believed it was always wrong to pay one group of people to peddle another group of richer people. The teacher knew nothing of this argument, and would probably have been surprised by its ferocity. He was proud that his grandfather had left the village and established his family in the capital of China, whatever the business. The teacher himself had benefited from that decision to move.

A look at some of the people we saw as we drove through the village seemed to suggest this was the right way of looking at things. We passed a scruffy middle-aged couple walking an equally scruffy-looking herd of goats. Both humans and animals wore the same downcast expression. A little further on, a group of young children played in the dirt. There seemed to be very little going on in the village. A sign on the door of what must have been a shop revealed that someone inside cut hair. The place looked so careworn that it was difficult to tell whether the salon was shut for the day or had closed down years ago. We didn't stay long. The teacher was still dressed as a woman and didn't want to get out in case someone recognised him. I thought there was little chance of that, but it showed just how nervous he was about what he wore around family. After driving up and down the main street a couple of times, he turned the car and we drove back to Beijing.

Spend, Spend, Spend

There's a remarkable photograph taken at the height of the Cultural Revolution that at first sight seems to offer little insight into the feelings of Chinese people at the time. It was shot by Li Zhensheng, a photojournalist working on the *Heilongjiang Daily* in the northern city of Harbin. His job allowed him to document the ebb and flow of the Cultural Revolution in the province where the teacher was sent to work. The photographer's black and white shots reveal the true brutality of the times. In one disturbing series of prints, the provincial governor, Li Fanwu, is shown having his hair hacked off in front of a crowd of baying people. He'd been accused of having political ambitions because his hairstyle was similar to Chairman Mao's, so local Red Guards chopped it off. The trimmings were stuffed into the top of his jacket and he was made to bow for hours while standing on a chair. Li Zhensheng disobeyed orders and kept the negatives of the shots he'd taken of the assault on the provincial governor. He hid them, along with hundreds of others, under the floorboards of his home. Decades later these rare photographs were printed in a book that reveals the absolute mayhem unleashed during the Cultural Revolution. The photographs of Li Fanwu encapsulate the cruelty of the time, but one day when I was looking through the pictures it was another, far less dramatic image that caught my eye.

The photograph that attracted my attention has none

of the hysteria on show in the chopping of the governor's hair. It shows a table set up in the stadium close to where he was being humiliated. The table is covered with a cloth and placed on top are several everyday items: three watches, two brooches and three fake leather handbags. These objects appear commonplace. They look like something someone might pick up from a second-hand store, but at the time these simple accessories were charged with political meaning. In the photograph taken by Li Zhensheng, the items have been carefully displayed on the table as proof of the provincial governor's crime of 'hoarding riches'. Li Fanwu's niece had been entrusted to look after this collection of objects, but had turned them over to the Red Guards, the teenagers stirred up by Mao to destroy the established political order. The photograph shows just how far to the left China had swung during the Cultural Revolution. Personal wealth and the pursuit of self-enrichment were grave political crimes. Perhaps more frightening, even simple items were evidence of this bourgeois sentiment. A watch nowadays seems proof of little more than a desire to know the time and perhaps, if the timepiece is expensive enough, it might suggest a little vanity, but back then it appeared to confirm extreme political unreliability.

China has changed almost beyond recognition since the picture was taken in 1966, both politically and materially. Back then, the possession of a fake leather handbag could result in terrible consequences, but China's nouveau riche would now be appalled at the affront to fashion. For many, only a genuine designer bag is an acceptable accessory. The world's premier fashion labels have all set up shop in China. Prada, Louis Vuitton and Dolce & Gabbana are probably as familiar now as the name Mao Zedong was back then. In Paris, London and Milan, Chinese tourists queue at shops selling the world's most luxurious and expensive goods.

187

No one would now look twice at the accessories captured through Li Zhensheng's lens. It's hard to believe that such everyday objects could ever inspire such anger; the politics that led to them being displayed on that table has now vanished. The photograph is also proof of something else: the ability of China's communist leaders to survive. They've moved from revolution to Rolex and from communism to Cartier without having to properly explain why.

Discussions about China's transformation over recent decades usually focus on the country's near-miraculous ability to make money. Change is measured in units of vehicles that come off the production line or in the number of new apartment blocks that have shot up like flowers in the spring rain, making fortunes for the real estate developers behind them. It's just as easy though to measure change by looking at how Chinese people spend their cash. Everyone likes to earn money, but we all get rid of it differently, and the differences give an insight into who we are.

In the 1970s, Chinese people had extremely limited consumer aspirations. That was partly because to cultivate them could get you into trouble, as the photograph of the fake leather handbags shows. It was also because there was not that much to buy and not a great deal of spare money to buy anything with. Chinese consumers – if such a concept even existed under Mao – coveted a series of simple items known helpfully as the *four big things*: a wristwatch, a bicycle, a sewing machine and a radio. China's economic reforms in the 1980s almost instantly led to an increase in people's disposable incomes, and so by the middle of the decade the *four big things* had been upgraded. A colour TV, a refrigerator, a stereo system and a washing machine were the must-have items. There seems to have been some disagreement as to exactly what by then constituted the *four big things*. A cassette recorder, an electric fan and a set of modern furniture also vied to be included on the list. This shows that even in the 1980s there was an expanding number of consumer durables on the market. As the decades rolled by, people would informally update the *four big things* to reflect the ever-increasing choice of goods on sale and mounting incomes that allowed people to buy them. By the noughties more affluent Chinese citizens could talk of getting an apartment, an expensive German car or going on an exotic holiday. It became clear that as in other wealthy countries, four things hardly cover the range of items we now think we want. The time when a watch was the height of desirability in China has long gone.

Like everyone else, the teacher was caught up in this wave of buying. Among his papers I found an article he'd written about a time in the early 1990s when his family had their first telephone installed. It's a tender piece of writing that recalls a period in China, not that long ago, when even a small purchase could lead to great excitement. It reminds us of more innocent times, when consumers were not yet jaded by the sheer number and variety of things to buy.

Thank goodness! We applied for a telephone ages ago and finally, just before the end of the year, we were connected. I clasped my two hands together and bowed three times. We had a telephone and everyone was happy. My father said: 'Previously, only the families of big officials could get a phone – now everyone can have one.' Even my four-year-old son said he was willing to take calls. No one could stop looking at the red telephone that we'd placed on a tea table. A colleague of mine kept coming round to 'test' it was still working and my wife stayed off work with a made-up illness, just to revel in the joy of our new telephone. She called all our friends and family to give them the glad tidings. She also bought a special book so we could take down notes when people rang.

Being constantly contactable does have its drawbacks, as the teacher and his family soon discovered.

> In the following days we took a lot of calls. Once I was cooking dinner when someone rang. My son answered. 'Who are you looking for?' he shouted down the receiver. He talked like a real adult. Afterwards, we'd just sat down to eat when the telephone rang again. My wife put down her chopsticks and went to answer. She ended up chatting for 20 minutes. After we'd eaten I laid down on the bed, but before long my son called out. 'Dad, someone wants you.' I didn't get round to finishing all the little things I was supposed to do that day. Another time, the phone rang so early that it startled both me and my wife. It was a wrong number from a night owl. After just a few days my wife could hardly stand it. 'Having a telephone is supposed to be convenient, but its constant ringing is so annoying.'

It's almost impossible to overstate the material benefits that have flowed from China's economic transformation. Reading the teacher's article about his family's first telephone brought to mind the story of the mother of Madam Fu, the former Chinese ambassador to Britain. She'd hoarded ration coupons used to buy rice and noodles, but now it's not unusual for middle-class Chinese people to go on holiday to Bali or Hawaii. Then there are those with the kind of wealth that previously only the emperors of China could lay their hands on. Many of these ultra-wealthy people keep a low profile, perhaps afraid that their money might attract envy or an investigation from the authorities into their tax affairs. It wasn't always easy to talk to them. But sometimes a journalist gets lucky and during one ordinary-sounding interview with a Chinese industrialist, I got an unexpected insight into the desires and aspirations of this wealthy elite.

Ding Liguo made his money in steel and ran his empire from an eight-storey office building on the outskirts of Beijing. When my colleagues and I arrived for the interview, Mr Ding was in a meeting, so his assistant showed us up to the top floor to wait. It was clearly a place to relax. There were comfy sofas dotted here and there, art on the walls and bottles of expensive spirits lined up in racks. I'd just settled down in a large armchair when I heard a familiar but unexpected sound, then caught a whiff of burning incense. The sound was a Buddhist monk chanting nearby, something I'd heard in the mountains of Tibet, but didn't think I'd come across in the rather sterile environment of a modern office block. I stood up and began looking round, wondering where this hypnotic noise was coming from. After a short search, I stumbled upon a tiny mock-up of a Buddhist monastery, with a young Tibetan monk sitting inside. He was singing softly and occasionally tapping together two small cymbals. I found out later that the monk had been hired by Mr Ding, one of China's most successful entrepreneurs, to sit there and chant. The businessman liked to pop up to the eighth floor every now and then to be reminded of a more spiritual way of life.

I'd never met anyone with their own monk before, so I was keen to talk to Mr Ding. When I interviewed him, his fortune was measured in hundreds of millions and he was a member of China's parliament, so he was obviously a person of some consequence who no doubt made tough decisions daily. But the steelmaker had another side to his personality, one he allowed me to glimpse when the camera stopped rolling. Journalists often pick up the most interesting pieces of information when a formal interview is over. Interviewees who, up until then, have been careful with their answers suddenly relax. They seem to forget to whom they are still talking and speak more freely. So it turned out with Mr Ding. He invited me and my colleagues to stay for lunch. I was intrigued. What would a multi-millionaire serve up? The food was delivered promptly to the eighth floor on metal trays, which looked a little like something prison inmates might use. Each tray had a number of indentations, into which small portions of simple food had been ladled: tofu, vegetables and rice. Good food, but not expensive fare. I might have been eating at a work canteen.

Mr Ding is a Buddhist and started lunch with a prayer. As we ate, he made it clear that material wealth was not everything. He saw it as his role as a politician to promote a better way of living. I was interviewing him about a campaign he'd become involved in to persuade Chinese people to stop eating shark's fin soup, a tradition that's quickly working its way through the world's shark population. 'So much killing,' said Mr Ding, 'is upsetting the balance of nature.' Shark's fin soup is expensive and often ordered by people who want to show their guests just how much money they have. It's an attitude the steel man found distasteful. As Mr Ding talked, he reminded me of the kind of leader Confucius thought was best suited to govern. The philosopher believed the greatest rulers were the ones who set a moral example to those below them. It's an idea that can sound odd to Westerners, who tend to believe our leaders are no better than everyone else – and sometimes a little worse – when it comes to morality. I considered this Confucian ideal patronising, but Mr Ding certainly seemed to have been cast in this mould. He talked about how the elite should set a good example. Unfortunately, he said, many of China's newly rich did not know how to act. He hoped that would change. But Mr Ding's tastes were not as monkish as his conversation sometimes implied.

After lunch, he invited us down to his private office, two floors below. It had thick carpets and a comfortable bedroom for Mr Ding when he worked late. There were display cases containing expensive antiques, including a large model of a horse. It was one thousand years old. There was also a suit of armour from the Ming dynasty, an era that ended in the early seventeenth century. Mr Ding jabbed his finger in delight in the direction of the delicate leather straps attached to the metal of the armour. They were still there, intact, after all this time. It was history I could touch, if only there hadn't been a pane of glass separating me from this valuable relic from the past. Framed photographs of Mr Ding's family adorned a side table. He told me he had five children. At the time, China's draconian family planning policies still restricted most couples to just one child. Even now, most can have only two. I wondered how Mr Ding had managed to circumvent a law that would have brought severe consequences for most other people, but I was a little afraid to ask. He'd invited me into his office and I didn't feel comfortable challenging him on that point.

I did ask about his children's education though. It turned out that some of Mr Ding's offspring went to Harrow, an international school in Beijing linked to the famous private school in Britain. His eldest was about to go to university in America. Mr Ding, it seemed, preferred to trust foreigners with his children's education. Chinese citizens often have complicated feelings towards the West, especially when it comes to countries that in the past forced China into unequal colonial arrangements, nations such as Britain, France and the United States. People are often extremely critical of these countries. Some go further, believing Western nations want to stop what many Chinese citizens see as their country's natural and peaceful rise to power and prosperity. Quite often these same people also harbour enormous, if grudging, respect for the world's more developed countries. Many love the US and are awed by its strength and vitality. It didn't surprise me that Mr Ding wanted to send his child to university in America. After all, the country's leader, Xi Jinping, sent his own daughter to Harvard. Mr Ding told me that China's rich needed to learn from the West. He obviously wanted to start that process with his own children.

After years of poverty it sometimes seemed as if everyone in China was on a spending spree. Who could blame them for splashing out when many had worried away large chunks of their lives trying to work out where the next meal would come from? I often talked to the teacher about this subject and so he suggested we go on a trip to Shandong province to see some of his wife's relatives. They'd spent the last few years working hard and spending hard. He thought they were just the kind of people I should meet.

We decided to drive to Shandong in the teacher's dull but sturdy Toyota sedan. I remembered what his driving had been like when we'd visited his former homestay business. It wasn't an experience I wanted to repeat. At the wheel, he seemed unsure about the difference between the brake and the accelerator, and readily admitted that his poor eyesight made it difficult for him to see where he was going. I decided that if we were going to drive anywhere again I would have to be in control, even though that meant I had to take a written test to qualify for a Chinese driving licence. It took me hours to learn about all the different road signs, bylaws and protocols, but I considered it a price worth paying.

On the day we left we set off early. The teacher was again dressed as a woman for our trip outside the capital. I now suspected that he'd agreed to travel with me across China partly because it gave him the opportunity to wear female clothes. I didn't mind. I was now completely comfortable with his feminine self, but couldn't help smiling at his tight yellow T-shirt. Printed on it were two ice cream cones with the words 'sweet treat' written in English above them. The plan was to drive to somewhere near the relatives' coastal town and visit them the following day. We made good time. China's economic growth has been built partly on government infrastructure spending: roads, high-speed railways and airports, but some of these projects were completed before people were ready to take advantage of them, and this seemed to be the case with the motorway to Shandong. It was nearly empty. The vehicles that were travelling in our direction seemed to prefer local roads, for which there were no tolls.

Our rapid progress meant we could now visit the relatives that evening, instead of the following day, but that left the teacher with a problem: he didn't want to appear in front of them dressed as a woman. A high-speed change was in order, so while I was still overtaking a slow-moving truck he unbuckled his seatbelt and dived into the back. As we sped along I kept getting glimpses of an arm or a leg in my rear-view mirror, as he peeled off one set of clothing and replaced it with another. His 'sweet treat' T-shirt was put away for another day in favour of a plain black one he thought looked less feminine. When he'd finished, he climbed back into the front seat. He asked me to stop at the next service station so he could dash into the toilets and wipe off his make-up. When we finally got to our destination and stepped out of the car, the teacher appeared to have retained only one item of clothing from his previous get-up. On his feet he wore something that was a cross between socks and tights; short, like socks, but made of nylon like tights. No one else seemed to notice them, possibly because many Chinese men wear something similar.

We stopped first at the house of the eighty-nine-year-old woman who was the head of the family. Her three adult children had come from their nearby homes to greet us.

They all lived in town, but it was a small town so they were excited about the arrival of a relative from China's great capital city. The teacher and the matriarch's youngest son immediately began a debate about cars and set off on a tour of the Toyota we'd just arrived in. The two men kicked tyres and admired the bodywork, before doing the same with the youngest son's Buick. They muttered compliments about each other's vehicles, and both seemed happy that the other was showing so much interest. I knew the teacher didn't know much about cars and wasn't particularly interested in how they looked, but it was a chance for both men to show off a little.

I was also struck by the fact that this was a very masculine activity. It hit me because most of the time the teacher and I had been on the road he'd been dressed as a woman and had been free to show off his feminine side, but among family he was more cautious. I didn't ask him about it, but presumed it would have been awkward to explain his cross-dressing to people who might not understand, and whom he would have to keep meeting year after year. I knew that inside the boot of his car he kept a holdall containing dozens of items of women's clothing. 'It's the best place to keep them,' he once told me. 'In there, they're out of the way.' Of course, he didn't tell the Shandong family about the bag of clothes, where the trappings of his other life were neatly packed and out of sight.

When we finally went indoors, the talk turned to new houses. The youngest son was buying an apartment right behind his mother's single-storey courtyard home, where we were sitting drinking tea. Looking round, I could see why so many people in China dream of a new home with all mod cons. The house we were crammed into consisted of just two rooms. One room was dominated by a *kang*, a large stone bed with a fire underneath, just like the one the teacher had slept on in Ao'bao Mountain. It was the home's only source of heating. In the summer, when we visited, Shandong is sunny and warm, but the winters can be fiercely cold. The elderly woman who lived in this badly insulated home must have spent many winter months on her bed huddled under a thick quilt. The house was typical of the homes that many poor people in China still live in. Water came from a tap in the courtyard and there was very little in the way of furnishing. A collection of framed family photographs seemed to be the most prized possessions. No one could describe the house as comfortable.

The home did have some charm. It was tiny and had been built for someone without much money, but the builder who'd put it up had obviously thought the occupants deserved a little splendour. A high wall surrounded the courtyard at the front of the house and there was an impressive entranceway. It had a tiled roof that swept up at either end, mimicking the architecture of Beijing's Forbidden City, which had once been home to China's emperors. A beautiful rural scene had been painted above the doorway and the solid wooden door looked as though it could repel even determined invaders. Pasted to it were good luck slogans painted on bright red strips of paper. They'd been put up for China's New Year celebrations and fortunately no one had bothered to take them down. The bright red glinted in the sunlight, suggesting fun was to be had inside. The courtyard was decked with plants, many of which were in flower, and when we arrived the elderly woman who lived there was sitting out in the sunshine chatting to a neighbour. This cannot have been an easy task because the family matriarch had false teeth – both top and bottom – that were far too large. They kept falling out of her mouth when she spoke, making it almost impossible for me to understand what she was saying. Dentistry has a long way to go in China.

I was beginning to see the old woman's house in a different light when the youngest son and his wife asked me and the teacher to go around the corner and see their new apartment. It was part of a recently started development that would eventually be home to hundreds of people, but the youngest son's flat was at that moment just a concrete shell surrounded by scaffolding. We ignored the safety signs that warned people to keep out of the building site and picked our way up to the second floor of a block towards the back. The new home was still a dark and dirty empty space, but the son's wife took us through rooms that would soon be packed with consumer goodies. She was obviously excited and explained what each area would be used for. 'I'm going to put the dining table here,' she said, pointing to a spot next to a large unglazed window. I looked out through the open space and saw the sun was just setting. I thought a dining table by the window might eventually be a nice place to sit and think about life.

On the ground floor, the couple had bought a garage for their Buick and extra storage space for the items they couldn't fit into their new home. They were living the dream, one that they'd been encouraged to pursue by their government. Property rights are still in their infancy in China, and it's not always clear who owns what and for how long, but officials constantly promote home ownership. These bureaucrats want even rural people to live in blocks of flats. They see it as the epitome of modern living. The new apartment the teacher and I were being shown round would obviously be wonderful when completed, but lifestyles would have to change if everyone lived several storeys up. There wouldn't be as much space for plants and it wouldn't be as easy to sit chatting to neighbours in the sun. Not everything would change for the better.

That evening the teacher's relatives took us out for a meal

at a local restaurant. We ate in a private dining room upstairs and, as is now often the case in China, it was a banquet that would have graced any special occasion. When the meal was over and everyone was talking, I slipped away and went downstairs to pay the bill. We were being treated well and I wanted to show my appreciation. By that time I'd lived in China for many years and should have known it was the wrong thing to do. Didn't I realise that by paying the bill my hosts would lose 'face'?

'Face' is a concept that's pivotal to Chinese life. It broadly translates as 'honour' or 'respect' and is familiar to people across the world, but its importance in China is probably greater than in any other country. The possibility of losing face is ever present in most social interactions, as I knew only too well. I'd had a stark reminder of that when I'd gone to interview a group of pensioners who gathered every morning in a Beijing park to chat and exercise. They practised tai chi, flew kites and walked backwards, an unusual exercise many older people engage in because they believe it's more arduous, and so more of a workout, than walking forwards. It also requires more thought and is supposed to ward off dementia. Pensioners meet in open spaces every day across the country and I went to the Beijing park to find out why they did it.

The old people I interviewed were not walking – either backwards or forwards – but playing table tennis on two public tables that had been installed near the park walls. I did my interviews and headed back to the BBC office, but before I'd left the park I realised I'd forgotten to take a photograph of one particular man I'd spoken to, so I went back. When I arrived, the man was no longer playing ping pong. There were only two tables and others were taking their turn. I needed him swishing his bat for the photograph though, so I asked one of the others if the man could play again while

I took his picture. He reluctantly agreed. Unfortunately, the man whose photograph I wanted began to enjoy being in front of the camera. 'Look at that great shot,' he would say as he sent the ball spinning to the other side of the table.

This annoyed the man who had stepped aside. He'd given up his spot on the table tennis table and was now having his nose rubbed in it by a show-off. The two elderly men exchanged angry words and before I could do anything about it they were nose-to-nose. Confrontations are slow to start in China, but difficult to stop once they get going. No one wants to back down, no one wants to 'lose face'. The men started shouting and hitting each other with their ping pong bats. I tried to intervene, explaining that it was all my fault, but no one was listening. More and more people joined the argument and in the end I had no choice but to leave them to it. I'd got more than a series of interviews that morning; I'd had a lesson in 'face'.

When the Shandong family realised that I'd paid the bill they were annoyed. They were the hosts and wanted to pay. They even started what I hoped was a good-natured argument with the restaurant manager, shouting at him for allowing me to settle the account. It was very important for them to treat their visitors from Beijing as esteemed guests, and for us in turn to respect their position as hosts. I'd unintentionally trampled on that convention.

The following day we visited the elder brother at his pig farm. It was a grim place. Large sows were laid on their sides in tiny pens, as hundreds of piglets pushed and shoved to get some milk. The farm had a stench that took a long time to forget. I didn't want to stay inside the sheds too long, and in any case I was mainly interested in getting a look at the brother, who seemed quieter than his siblings. The teacher told me that he was a shrewd man and the two had previously done some business together. They'd once shared ownership of a house in Beijing. Part of the teacher's wealth came from owning homes. Over the years he'd often talked about his attempts to secure his financial future and most of that seemed to be tied up in property. I liked listening to these stories because in China so much was being earned by so many. I wanted to know how they did it. Many people undoubtedly worked hard for their money, but in other cases success appeared to be down to sheer luck; being in the right place at the right time. That's how it seemed with the teacher, who'd already shown with his homestay business that finance was not his strong point. The *hutong* home he'd once owned with the Shandong brother, near Beijing's famous Temple of Heaven, seemed to encapsulate some of the good fortune the teacher enjoyed in later life.

Hutongs are the narrow alleyways that once crisscrossed the whole of Beijing. Behind their high walls hide the capital's traditional courtyard homes. The city's tourism bosses encourage visitors to seek out the tranquil beauty of this unique architectural heritage, but other branches of the urban government are less impressed, and have been tearing *hutongs* down at a tremendous pace. They might look pretty, but they are an inefficient way to house the capital's ever-expanding population. Most are just one storey high and the temptation to replace them with tower blocks has proved too great to resist. The result is that most *hutongs*, like the teacher's Alley of One Hundred Children, have now gone. This development has not only provided more housing, but also allowed everyone involved in the rebuilding process to benefit from a financial windfall, including the occupants or owners of the original courtyard homes.

The teacher had bought his stake in the *hutong* courtyard near the Temple of Heaven more than a decade before. The elder Shandong brother had originally owned it and had wanted to sell, but the teacher persuaded him not to, instead buying half for himself. The two parties put in tenants and shared the small annual rental income. Then along came a real estate company that had been given permission to redevelop the area. Residents were forced to move, as they inevitably are in China; there are never any long drawn-out legal battles over ownership. In any case, the teacher would not have been one of those arguing to stay. He couldn't believe his luck. A relatively small cash investment had now yielded a haul nearly ten times bigger than his original outlay. What's more, the developer also gave him two flats in the complex that was soon to be built on the vacant land. Good luck like this doesn't come along every day, not even every generation. The teacher had found himself with a valuable asset that he'd done little to merit, but as life had so often been unkind he was not going to feel too bad about a sudden shift in fortune. The Shandong brother received the same financial compensation as the teacher, a bonanza he kept from the rest of his family.

The teacher had other side deals that seemed to bring in an income, which meant that by the time I knew him he was comfortably off. His financial problems in later life were about how to spend money, not how to get it. In retirement, he dealt with a completely different set of monetary issues than those he'd grappled with as a young man. It was clear the teacher also realised, like many others before him, that financial security does not solve all of life's problems. He had an apartment, a car and a kitchen full of food, but he still yearned for something else. To satisfy this need for something more, he turned his thoughts to the countryside. Like many Chinese intellectuals before him, he hankered after a simpler way of life in a rural setting. This ideal has been expressed down the ages in poetry, painting and calligraphy. It's based on the Chinese belief that something might be gained by observing a bare rock or the blossom of a tree in spring. The teacher showed his appreciation of this age-old tradition by getting an allotment, which he'd once taken me to see.

His rural idyll was situated on the southern outskirts of Beijing at a place called Happy Farm. Middle-class people like the teacher would mostly visit at the weekends. He had a small plot, just 35 square metres. His name was written on one of the posts that marked its boundary. The teacher grew watermelons, green beans and cucumbers. The company that rented out the allotments had installed CCTV cameras overlooking each plot of land, so gardeners could go online in their city homes and see just how well their vegetables were progressing. I was just marvelling at this technological innovation when I noticed a man buzzing about the teacher's allotment. 'Who's he?' I whispered. It turned out the man was a migrant worker from a poor inland province who was paid by those who rented the allotments, including the teacher, to do the actual work. 'You mean you don't do it yourself?' I asked. 'Not often,' came the teacher's reply. 'I like coming here to pick the vegetables, but it's too hard work growing them.' I was momentarily lost for words, before guessing that the ancient Chinese poets who praised rural life probably didn't do the heavy lifting on their farms either. Once we'd had a good look at the work being done by the migrant worker, the teacher and I retired to a rest area, where we had a cooling drink and played snooker on an outdoor table. Later, the teacher wandered off to wash his car before taking me to Happy Farm's own restaurant for a sumptuous meal. The vegetables were supposed to have been grown on the allotments, but who knew for sure?

After the pig farm, the youngest son and his wife took us on a tour of the area in their Buick. Everywhere in this coastal region were signs of the industry that's making China rich. Hundreds of fishing vessels tied up in harbours spoke of people who still made their living from the sea, but the water also delivered something more precious: oil. The area has become a distribution point for fuel shipped in from across the world, brought to the ports of Shandong and then taken by truck to other parts of the country. As we drove along broken roads we passed long lines of trucks waiting to load up. It's a business the youngest son knows something about; he was the owner of several lorries himself. He didn't drive them personally; he employed others, who were at that moment somewhere nearby loading a consignment of marble. The youngest son knew exactly where they were because he'd installed GPS devices in each cab, so he could keep a close eye on things. I didn't have to ask him if he was doing well. His car, his new home and his plans for the future were sufficient indications. Like his older brother, he also had the generous waistline of a man who could afford three good meals a day.

Those who make money also want to spend it, and further along the coast there was a beach, where dozens of bathers were enjoying a little leisure. A hotel had been hastily erected near the shoreline to service their needs, and there were speedboats, sailboats and four-wheel-drive sand vehicles to hire. A heavy smog, perhaps caused by the construction of a new coal-fired power station nearby, meant it was difficult to see too far out to sea, but that didn't seem to bother the swimmers. Next door to the beach a large complex of apartment blocks was under construction. They were holiday homes aimed at out-of-towners, mostly elderly people who wanted to come to Shandong for the summer months. In the salesroom, an attractive young woman stood over a model of the proposed new development, explaining to potential buyers the advantages of owning a home by the sea. She handed out glossy brochures that included a handy map showing just how easy it was to travel to Shandong from

Beijing. The saleswoman was selling dreams, which came with one, two or three bedrooms. Some had sea views, but there were cheaper ones further away from the shoreline for those on a tighter budget. The assistant urged those listening not to dally, as the flats were being quickly snapped up.

Epilogue: London

When we left China, the teacher offered to drive me and my family to the airport, but we were taking back far more than we'd brought. I'd arrived in Beijing with my wife, our baby son and a couple of average-sized suitcases. I was leaving with two children and a large collection of items acquired over more than seven years of life in China. Some of our belongings were already on their way back to Britain in a container on board a ship, but we still had too many suitcases, bags and people for the teacher's Toyota to handle. I declined his offer and, having seen him for dinner a few weeks before, said a final goodbye on the phone. It was a rather muted and unsatisfactory ending to our colourful travels across China and through his life.

We left for many reasons, some big, some small. The pollution was a major factor. Like most foreigners who live in China, my wife and I were becoming increasingly concerned about the health of our children as they grew up in smoggy Beijing, not to mention our own wellbeing. Chinese parents are worried too, but most don't have the option of leaving. The full extent of the damage caused to people's bodies by living in China is not something that's easy to find out; the government keeps secret the number of people who die each year from pollution-related illnesses. Chinese citizens would probably panic if they knew the full facts. There were other issues that led to the decision to pack up and go. Many of them were minor, things that had built up after years of living in a bureaucratic country where even simple tasks can be difficult to complete. I'd become far too expert at arguing with officials, security guards and bank tellers.

There were deeper reasons for leaving that were harder to pin down. In some respects, I was beginning to dislike myself. To be a foreign journalist in China is to constantly pit yourself against the government and it was making me angrier than I wanted to be. They'd say 'black', we'd say 'white'. It was draining. I'd become disappointed with a government that was paranoid and devious. I thought Chinese people deserved something better. If being in China had taught me one thing, it's that there are other ways to live a life. Instead of professing to be so sure of themselves, I thought China's senior leaders should take on board that message themselves. For all their achievements, there are more civilised ways to run a country.

I was sad to be leaving so many friends, particularly the teacher, and I was disappointed that our farewell had not been more significant. But a year or so after arriving back in Britain I received an unexpected phone call. It was the teacher and he was excited. He and his wife had booked themselves on a tour of Europe that included a brief stopover in London. Could I meet them?

The unpredictability of our trips around China followed us to Britain. I was supposed to join the tour party at a restaurant in London's Chinatown. The group had only just left China, but they were already craving the food of home. Unfortunately, they never got into central London. A march had clogged up dozens of roads and traffic had come to a virtual standstill. The teacher's tour leader had decided to head straight to the hotel, way out in Hemel Hempstead, a distant commuter town. The coach was at that moment edging its way through the capital's congested streets. I realised that I might not get to see the teacher after all, so I decided to take matters into my own hands.

I'd been following the teacher's slow progress through London on a crackly telephone line. I got him to hand the mobile to the bus driver, a Polish man with a limited grasp of English. 'Tell me exactly where you are?' I shouted down the phone. 'Which direction are you travelling in and how fast are you moving? What colour is your bus?' The visitors were in a white coach on a road that runs alongside the north bank of the River Thames. They were heading west at walking pace. I tightened the straps of my rucksack and began to run, weaving in and out of meandering tourists and stationary vehicles.

I'd not run so fast in a long time and was gasping for breath when I got to the river. As I'd been running, I'd tried to calculate how far the bus would have travelled in the time it had taken me to get there. I went to the furthest point I thought it could have got to and started walking back down the road, scanning the traffic for white coaches and Chinese faces. It wasn't long before I found the right bus. The teacher was standing at the front next to the driver, peering at unfamiliar surroundings, looking for me. When we saw each other the driver opened the door and the teacher and I embraced, a little awkwardly, on the roadside. It was good to see him.

We talked excitedly about what we'd both been doing in the intervening period. We hadn't spoken much on the telephone since I'd left China so we had a lot to talk about. 'Your Chinese has gone backwards,' he said after a short while. I'd forgotten how blunt he could sometimes be. He didn't mean it as an insult; he was merely stating a fact. The teacher was with his wife and so was dressed as a man. There was nothing about his attire that even hinted at his other passion. I didn't bother to mention his clothes. Why would I? I'd come to realise a long time before that what he wore was irrelevant. Dressed as a man or dressed as a woman, he was always the teacher.

I'd been thinking a lot about identity and how we express ourselves. What did dressing in drag mean? The origin of the word is contested, but it seems to have started life in the Victorian theatre, where male actors would sometimes dress as women. They often wore long skirts that would 'drag' on the floor and so the word became associated with cross-dressing, particularly men made up to look like women. The word seems to carry the idea that those dressing up are pretending to be someone else, and I realised that with the teacher this wasn't true. Different aspects of his personality would emerge depending on whether he was wearing men's or women's clothing, but he was always himself. In fact, he sometimes seemed more true to his character when dressed as a woman. On our travels he'd put on female clothes whenever he could; he didn't wear them only when he knew it would create difficulties he wanted to avoid. To some extent, he was pretending when he dressed as a man.

There'd been others who'd pretended far more in China, mostly government officials. They often argue their homeland is something it's not. They trumpet the many successes, but sweep much of the bad stuff under the carpet. How can anywhere claim to be truly open and honest if a famine that killed tens of millions within living memory is off limits for proper discussion? If we're talking about pretence, sometimes it's China that's in drag.

When the tour bus finally hit the outskirts of London, the Chinese visitors had already been travelling for more than a day and had left London's Heathrow Airport several hours before. I know many Chinese people who suffer from travel sickness, particularly on buses, and looking round I could see some pasty faces. The teacher was one of those feeling ill and he indicated he wanted to be sick. His wife urged him to hold on. It seemed to take forever to get to the Holiday Inn in Hemel Hempstead. It was billed as a London hotel, but even members of the Chinese tour party, none of whom had ever been to Britain before, could see that this was something of an exaggeration. When we finally pulled up outside the hotel, the group staggered off the bus like a party of drunks.

As soon as he got on firm ground, the teacher put his fingers down his throat and tried to make himself sick. He made a terrible sound as he retched, but nothing would come up. Others did the same. A few more cleared their throats of phlegm. I looked round and saw that we'd pulled up by the large windows of the hotel restaurant. It seemed full. As they pushed food into their mouths, the diners looked down at the scene unfolding before them. Was I imagining it or did several put down their knives and forks? The Chinese government has become paranoid about how its citizens act abroad following a series of embarrassing incidents. Officials even produced a booklet that gives helpful advice for travelling overseas. 'Don't spit phlegm or gum, throw litter, urinate or defecate wherever you feel like it. Don't cough, sneeze or pick your nose or teeth in front of others,' urges one section of the book. I knew it wasn't their fault, but this Chinese tour group seemed to have broken a number of those rules already. I put my hand on the teacher's back to comfort him and tried not to look up again at the restaurant.

The next day the teacher had recovered. His tour party made a bewildering sprint around southern England. They went to Oxford then Windsor and ended up back again in central London. I'd left them on the previous evening and caught up with them again outside Buckingham Palace. They peered through the iron railings and wondered aloud whether the Queen was at home. 'Everything's so old,' said the teacher. In China, the words 'modern' and 'wealthy' have become synonymous with 'new'. The teacher was puzzled as to why a developed country such as Britain could have so many old buildings.

Later on, we finally got to Chinatown for a familiar meal. We were ushered into the back room of a restaurant to eat a different kind of food to the fare being served out front. I was the only Westerner in the group and the tourists piled my plate with the tastiest morsels. I'd almost forgotten how polite Chinese people could be, but there was little time to savour the food. The tour guide was hurrying people out of the restaurant while they were still chewing, reminding them there was a tight schedule to keep. I couldn't help thinking about the whistle-stop tour the teacher and I had taken in Chairman Mao's hometown back in China.

In a matter of minutes, they were preparing to leave. The tour guide had managed to get almost everyone back onto the bus without too much fuss. I wasn't going with them so I quickly hugged the teacher and said goodbye before he clambered aboard. I thought it might be the last time I saw him for a while. He found his seat and waved through the window as the bus pulled away from the kerb. I wanted to thank him for taking me around China and helping me understand its people. He'd shown me traits that were not always obvious: tolerance, humour and determination. I'd learned that Chinese people usually try to make the best of whatever life throws at them. Times had been tough, but things are now getting better and, if this one tour group was anything to go by, people are keen to enjoy themselves. I wanted to say all that and more, but by the time I'd thought it through properly the bus was already gone and the teacher had disappeared from view.

Acknowledgements

Thanks to Vincent Ni and Roy Kibbler, both of whom patiently read this book and gave good advice, and of course thanks to everyone in China who took time to speak to me.

www.sandstonepress.com

facebook.com/SandstonePress/

@SandstonePress